Macro Marketing
A Social Perspective

The Wiley Marketing Series

Macro Marketing

A Social Perspective

REED MOYER

Michigan State University

John Wiley & Sons, Inc.

New York · London · Sydney · Toronto

Library of Congress Cataloging in Publication Data:

Moyer, Reed.
Macro marketing.

(The Wiley marketing series)
1. Marketing. I. Title.

HF5415.M678   380.1   72-630
ISBN 0-471-62109-9
ISBN 0-471-62110-2 (pbk.)

Printed in the United States of America

10 9 8 7 6 5 4 3 2 1

To my Mother and to the memory of my Father

Preface

The present is a questioning time in our history. Americans traditionally have challenged basic assumptions and modes of operations and have considered whether things can be improved. They scrutinize some ideas and institutions more than others. Traditional targets of criticism are business and marketing, and this criticism has an ancient lineage. For centuries man has suspected the trader and huckster and has feared the moneylender. Although Americans are not unique in their distrust of businessmen, they may look on him in a little friendlier fashion than others do. Charles Wilson's famous gaffe that "What's good for the country is good for General Motors and vice versa" raised the expected cry of outrageous indignation, but it found a sympathetic audience also.

The current wave of doubt, skepticism, and despair that afflicts the United States leads to a heightened questioning of our individual and collective goals, of our priorities and values, and of our institutions. It is understandable, therefore, that marketing, a prominent activity whose institutions serve our daily needs, experiences special scrutiny. This scrutiny intensifies the latent hostility toward commerce. Irritation derived from marketing's *perceived* performance undoubtedly contributes to the new wave of consumerism that is exemplified by Nader's Raiders, retail boycotts, and increased agitation for consumer protection legislation.

Increased consumer concern over marketing activities calls for an evaluation of marketing performance. This book makes that evaluation. It requires a different perspective from the usual marketing textbooks, which are firm-oriented and take a micro approach. The reader is usually shown how to improve the firm's marketing performance. He learns about pricing and pricing strategies, the uses of promotion, ways to gain control of distribution channels, techniques of assessing market opportunities, and the value of market planning. Although social implications of the firm's behavior may receive some attention, the books generally provide a managerial orientation.

This volume has a broader perspective. It focuses on larger societal issues related to marketing. Whereas the typical managerial marketing textbook is firm- or *micro*-oriented, this book is *macro*-oriented. That is, it analyzes marketing in a larger framework than the firm. It studies marketing within the context of the entire economic system, with special emphasis on its aggregate performance.

Here are specific examples that make the micro-macro distinction clearer. A firm decides to increase its advertising to achieve a specified goal: to increase market share or profits, for instance. This is a micro-level decision; it is made by the firm and its outcome directly affects the firm. However, an analysis of the impact on society of *all* advertising expenditures is a *macro* issue. So is an issue like efficiency. Micro analysis might deal with attempts of individual firms to reduce distribution costs, or it might study the effect on the firm of abandoning a retail location. At the macro level, emphasis shifts to the efficiency performance of the entire distributive sector or to the social and economic impact of the "wastes" from retail store mortality.

Macro marketing issues go beyond the above examples. They include such topics as the effectiveness of marketing in securing the needs of given sectors; for instance, ghetto residents, the whole range of public policy issues relating to regulations and legislation designed to promote product safety, provide market information, and regulate competition, and the broadest issue of all—marketing's roles in our complex socioeconomic system.

By studying the social impact of various marketing activities and weighing the contributions and deficiencies of marketing as an organized behavior system, the marketing manager is confronted with an evaluation that differs from the evaluation associated with micro analysis. Ordinarily he finds his performance measured in the context of the firm's goals of profit maximization, sales maximization, industry dominance, and so on. A macro perspective puts his behavior in a different light. It analyzes the combined impact on society of each marketer and determines whether marketing behavior and performance match society's needs and expectations.

I do not attempt to deal with every conceivable macro marketing issue. I ignore completely questions involving the changing structure of retail distribution and problems flowing from the need to create mass distribution systems to match systems of mass production. Instead, the book spotlights several key social and economic issues at the macro level.

One of my purposes here is to evaluate marketing's performance. How well does it perform its functions? How effectively does it respond to its challenges? Is it true that marketing creates "false" wants, manipulates men's minds, bamboozles innocent consumers, and wastes precious resources in duplicative advertising? We need to evaluate these and other charges to sift truth from unverified assertion.

The effective evaluation of marketing requires an understanding, first, of what functions it performs and how its activities have developed over time. Therefore, Chapter 1 examines marketing's role in simple economic systems and shows how its role broadens its functions as economies develop. Having laid this base, the book discusses various prominent marketing issues. The focus is on marketing activities and measures of marketing performance that have commanded considerable interest among both scholars and the average consumer. Thus, separate chapters are devoted to advertising, marketing efficiency, consumerism issues, and ghetto marketing.

In most subject areas I accomplish several things. First, I describe the phenomena under discussion. Also, when appropriate, I give pro and con viewpoints. Many marketing issues require this treatment because of their controversial nature. Marketing's adversaries criticize; its defenders rebut. Moderation often loses out to hyperbole. I try to avoid taking sides in the arguments. Instead, I serve as moderator by letting all voices be heard. When necessary I analyze the conflicting viewpoints and pose questions for the reader. The issues discussed and the questions raised will challenge the marketing student. They are topical, they lie at the heart of the discipline, and they have important social implications. In an era marked by unfettered passions, an illumination of the issues by dispassionate discussion will contribute to a better understanding of them.

This volume will serve several markets. First, it should appeal to any consumer who has thought about the important macro marketing issues that are analyzed here. Hopefully the elaboration of pro and con positions will help the thoughtful reader to become more aware of their complexity and will aid him in formulating rational value judgments. Students in courses in consumer economics, social issues, and public policy will also profit from this book.

Its greatest value, however, is its use as a supplement to managerially oriented marketing texts either at the introductory or intermediate level. Books such as E. J. McCarthy's *Basic Marketing: A Managerial Approach* and Philip Kotler's *Marketing Management: Analysis, Planning and Control* explain marketing from a viewpoint that will aid existing or future marketing managers; and they present useful ways of analyzing marketing problems and managing inputs to achieve marketing objectives. However, books of this type are predominantly firm-oriented, whereas students are clamoring for greater emphasis on the broader social, ethical, and economic issues that are discussed here. An instructor who assigns both a managerially oriented text and the present volume will give his students a balanced micro-macro mix that will

enrich the course and command greater student interest and involvement. Questions at the end of each chapter offer points for class and
small section discussions.

Reed Moyer

Contents

Macro Marketing
A Social Perspective

1

Marketing's Role in Society

Adam Smith's felicitous phrase concerning man's inherent tendency to "truck, barter and exchange" has settled, for many, the question of whether trade is an inevitable human process.[1] Recent studies of primitive societies, however, dispute this contention. Anthropologists further question whether the exchange system is the inevitable method of distributing goods.

Karl Polanyi indicates three ways to integrate primitive economies.[2] The market exchange system, with which we are familiar, is one; the others are systems of reciprocity and redistribution. Under reciprocity there is a two-way, circular flow of goods. With this system, each village has service groups (tailors, smiths, priests) which provide services for all members of the community and which, in return, receive grain and other crops grown by the farmers. Individuals' status, not their contributions, determines the shares they receive. This system still exists in many primitive regions of the world.

Redistribution "means that the produce of the group is brought together either physically or by appropriation, and then parcelled out again among the members."[3] The job of redistributing goods usually falls to a chief or some other authority figure in the community.

Neither of these systems performs what we characterize as marketing activities although they arrange for the exchange of goods and services. Marketing and price-determination occur in the market exchange system. This involves a multidirectional flow of goods and services, the values of which are expressed in terms of the things traded (i.e., barter) or in terms of another commodity (money price system).

[1] Much of the material in this section is drawn from the author's *Marketing in Economic Development* (International Business Occasional Paper #1, Institute for International Business Management Studies, Michigan State University, 1965, with permission.)

[2] Karl Polanyi, Conrad M. Arensberg, and Harry W. Pearson, *Trade and Markets in the Early Empires* (Glencoe, Ill.: The Free Press, 1957), p. 222.

[3] Leon V. Hirsch, *Marketing in an Underdeveloped Economy: The North Indian Sugar Industry* (Englewood Cliffs, N.J.: Prentice-Hall, 1961), p. 370.

The various segments of a total economic system never advance in lockstep. Backward regions exist even in highly developed systems. Likewise, within primitive economies, exchange systems of reciprocity and redistribution may coexist in the same community, each system applying to different commodities and different groups of inhabitants. In the emerging sectors of the economy, the market exchange system may be used. Even in the United States one finds all three systems at work. The majority of transactions, of course, use the market exchange principle. Public expenditures for education, welfare, and national defense exemplify the principle of redistribution. Gift exchanges are based largely on the principle of reciprocity.

In less-developed economies one finds varying degrees of dependence on markets and the market mechanism. "Market" refers to physical sites, that is, marketplaces where buyers and sellers meet to transact business. The "market mechanism" is a means of determining prices of goods and services through supply and demand forces. There are three classes of societies that rely on distinctly different types of markets and market mechanisms.[4]

First are societies with no marketplaces and only isolated instances of the market mechanism at work. These are typified by economies in which several transactional spheres exist (reciprocity, redistribution, market exchange).

In the second type of society, markets and market mechanisms exist but only peripherally. The community would suffer little if either were eliminated since it scarcely depends on them. These societies have two characteristics: market sales are not the principal means of providing for the members' material well-being and sellers of goods are what Bohannan and Dalton refer to as "target marketers." That is, sellers enter markets to achieve specific short-range targets—to earn income to cover a tax liability or to pay for a specific good.

In these tangential markets, prices are used not as a means of allocating resources but to indicate values of goods and services and to establish equivalences among them. The limited role of prices in primitive markets sharply contrasts with their dominant position in developed economies where prices serve as signals regulating resource allocation. In both types of economies—developed and underdeveloped—supply and demand forces determine prices in free markets. But in a primitive economic system characterized by peripheral markets, the

[4] Paul Bohannan and George Dalton derive the classification based on their experience in Africa. See their *Markets in Africa* (Evanston, Ill.: Northwestern University Press, 1962), pp. 1–8.

result of price formation is analogous to its effect in antique auction markets. Market forces determine antique auction prices, but their effect ends with the auction. There is no feedback to the rest of the economy to regulate the allocation of resources among various productive activities. Economies characterized by peripheral markets also lack this kind of feedback.

The third type of society has marketplaces and market mechanisms that integrate the economy, determine prices and income, and allocate resources. To develop, an economy must move away from the two primitive distribution systems and toward the third—a system of integrative markets. Only by substituting market exchange systems for systems embedded in tribal ritualism can the incentives that impel growth be fully provided. Paradoxically, the more an economy depends on the market mechanism, the less relative importance it attaches to the marketplace per se. Labor, land, and capital increasingly enter the market but not in marketplaces. The market for aluminum ingots, for example, may include the entire country although few of the ingots will move through physical market sites.

Whether or not trading arises spontaneously is open to question. A trade obviously involves decisions by two or more individuals to exchange goods to their mutual advantage. The incentive to trade could come from the pleasure derived from the act of trading itself. In fact, there is ample evidence that the opportunities for social intercourse stimulate interest in trading. But the utility derived from the social aspect of trading apparently is a by-product of the process and not its root cause. In its earliest stages, trading activity appears to stem from the pressures of population growth and land shortages and, occasionally, from the need to earn income to meet pressing obligations.

THE FUNCTIONS OF MARKETING □ The role of marketing in various stages of development is multidimensional. In early stages it performs a number of functions that aid the development process in several ways. What are some of these functions?

First, marketing performs an important organizational and informational function. When properly operating, it creates "a network through which information can flow among the many firm units performing interrelated activities necessary to produce the final consumer product."[5]

---

[5] Norman Collins, "Marketing and Economic Development: The Experience of Southern Italy" in a Report on the General Assembly of the Mediterranean Social Sciences Research Council, Cairo, U.A.R. December 1–5, 1962, p. 153.

Farm planting decisions, for example, cannot be made in a vacuum. Information is needed concerning the requirements of other links in the production-distribution channel; for example, the requirements of food processors, retailers, and final consumers. Organizing the information network and providing the physical facilities to handle the product system's output fall to the distributive sector. Its activities may be varied, ranging from the gauging of consumer demand and the standardization of product quality to the organization of physical distribution systems.

Of great importance is the function of equalizing and distributing goods from surplus to deficit areas under shifting demand and supply conditions. Any distribution system—primitive or advanced—faces certain common problems. Goods do not flow in equal amounts in a steady stream from producers to consumers, nor do consumers purchase at a constant rate an amount equal to the output of individual producers. The job of matching and equalizing diverse supplies and demands falls to the distributive sector. Implicit in the matching concept is the connective function of distribution. Any exchange system involves a linkage of geographically separated entities. The spatial connections may be as simple as the distribution of farm commodities in primitive village markets, or as complex as some of the distributive networks for nationally marketed goods in highly developed countries.

Additionally, the middleman performs what Westerfield calls the "capitalistic" functions.[6] The distributor deals in time markets. The uneven character of demand and supply conditions and the need to link surplus with deficit areas separated both spatially and temporally adds a speculative dimension to his job. Buying with temporally distant markets in view, the middleman assumes risks supportable only on a base of capital.

To carry out these functions, the distributor must perform certain activities. He must store goods and provide special facilities for commodities with unique characteristics, for example, perishable foodstuffs; he must provide a communication network; he must transport goods; he must provide credit facilities.

As a by-product of its activities, marketing may perform two important functions that aid the developmental process. These are the creation of pools of both entrepreneurial talent and capital. Although these activities occur continuously during the developmental process, the

---

[6] Bert Westerfield, *Middlemen in English Business* (New Haven: Yale University Press, 1915), p. 369.

impact of these developments is probably greatest during the period prior to commercial revolution, which Kindleberger views as "a vital and almost necessary step on the way to industrial revolution."[7] Studies of the origins of industrialists in developing countries find that a large share of them move into industry directly from trading occupations.

Why should trading be such a fertile field for developing industrial entrepreneurs? Adam Smith recognized the value of mercantile trading. "The habits . . . of order, economy, and attention," he said, "to which mercantile business naturally forms a merchant, render him much fitter to execute with profit and success, any project of improvement."[8] The willingness of traders to assume the risks inherent in trading stands them in good stead when faced with opportunities to enter the industrial field. Moreover, their contacts with consumers permit them to recognize the prevailing market opportunities better than most other members in the economy. Unlike artisans, employees, or landlords, traders are accustomed to buying and selling, to employing others, and to entering into contracts—experiences that prepare them for the responsibilities of operating industrial establishments. Later in this section we note the expanded role of marketing as societies move from a condition of scarcity to one of abundance. Along with this shift, the entrepreneurial function broadens to include more than just the creation of pools of entrepreneurial talent. It provides methods, programs, and systems of action that promote the firm's growth.

The extension of markets, through application of the connective principle previously discussed, permits scale economies. Trade links together local producer and local markets; local markets join to form regional markets; region connects to region, creating national markets. But the economies extend beyond those enjoyed by the primary and secondary industries whose goods the distributive sector is responsible for marketing. Just as industrial producers gain scale economies from the extension of their markets, so too do distributors. Increasing the scale of marketing operations produces economies in several ways: in the processing of orders, in conducting the contactual functions, and in the physical handling of commodities. Organized exchanges develop, and these create scale economies in the communication of market information. Routinization replaces the individual treatment of market transactions.

[7] Charles P. Kindleberger, *Economic Development* (New York: McGraw-Hill, 1958), p. 93.

[8] Adam Smith, *The Wealth of Nations* (New York: Modern Library Edition), p. 385.

Critics often charge marketing with being wasteful; still, the use of marketing intermediaries can economize resources in the sale of goods to consumers. Under a primitive, decentralized system, producers of various goods may exchange their surpluses directly with each other. Thus, in a system composed of six producers who are also consumers there will be fifteen transactions if each producer trades at least once with all of the other producers. Generalizing, there will be $[n(n-1)]/2$ exchanges where n is the number of producers. Trading goods through a central market, however, requires only six exchanges, one by each producer with the market intermediary. The ratio of advantage from using a central exchange is $(n-1)/2$.[9]

The same principle applies in a more complex world in which producers and consumers are two distinct groups of people. Figures 1–1 and

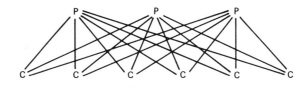

Figure 1–1

1–2 picture the transactions that occur among them, with and without the use of retailing intermediaries. In the first case, there are eighteen possible transactions among the three producers and six consumers if each consumer makes one purchase from each producer. Introducing a retailer into the system reduces the number of transactions to nine, three among producers and the retailer and six among the retailer and the consumers. This is a highly simplified example, but it is useful in establishing the economizing principle that is involved. The principle also applies to the use of other marketing intermediaries, for example, the interposition of wholesalers between producers and retailers.

As economies grow, the scope of marketing grows. Also, institutions necessary to perform them emerge, grow, and become modified by changing economic and social conditions.

[9] For an example of this analysis, see Wroe Alderson, "Factors Governing the Development of Marketing Channels," in Richard M. Clewett (ed.), *Marketing Channels* (Homewood, Ill.: Richard D. Irwin, 1954), pp. 7–8.

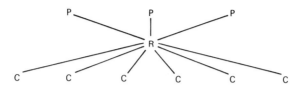

Figure 1–2

Agricultural production dominates the economies of countries in early stages of growth. Thus, marketing institutions needed to distribute agricultural commodities play a large role in the distribution system. Also, the functions are performed to facilitate agricultural activities. Communications will be more concerned with the dissemination of farm price and supply information than with the use of high-powered advertising techniques to sell consumer goods. With economic growth comes a relative change of emphasis away from agriculture and toward industrial goods production, thence toward the production of consumer goods and services. These changes create demands for new channels of distribution and different relative emphases on selling and advertising. Similarly, the trend toward urbanization that accompanies economic growth modifies channels of distribution, storage locations and arrangements, communications media used, and the transportation network that serves the changing markets.

Most of the discussion to this point deals with marketing's role in early stages of an economy's development. As the economy grows, marketing functions arise that facilitate getting goods from producer to consumer. These functions include buying, selling, storage, financing, risk-bearing, communication, standardization and grading, and transportation. It is a mistake, however, to conceive of marketing in a modern society as being limited to these functions on the one hand or necessarily including all of them on the other. Thus, the marketing of services may be performed without use of functions associated with physical production, for example, storage, grading, and transportation and so on.

Limiting the conception of marketing in a modern society (especially the United States) to the functions listed above falls short of reality. The modern marketing concept places marketing at the center of the entire business. Under this conception, marketing is more than a collection of functions; it is viewed as a corporate philosophy. The firm begins with the market and works back to production. The initial step involves assessing consumers' needs and then fashioning products and services to satisfy them. Thus, marketing activity begins before the sale. But it continues after the sale as activities which deliver satisfactory performance of purchased products and which provide feedback to improve marketing performance. Thus marketing is concerned with pretransactional, transactional, and posttransactional phases of a product or service's delivery to a customer.

The foregoing analysis of marketing's broadened conception in a modern economy stresses the pretransactional assessment of market needs. But the process involves more than this. An economy such as that of the United States long ago passed from a condition of scarcity to one of abundance. We created and mastered mass production techniques that provided an outpouring of low-cost goods in increasing amounts. But the advent of mass production required a concomitant development of mass distribution techniques and facilities. The task of matching mass production with mass distribution fell to marketers. Since this is a dynamic process, the job of continually adjusting marketing functions and institutions to the growth of aggregate output goes on.

Another aspect of the shift from an economy of scarcity to one of abundance is the need for marketers to stimulate demand for new products and services. Once production provides for satisfying basic needs, growth relies progressively upon the demand-stimulating activity of marketing. (Later we shall deal with the issue of the desirability of growth as a social and economic goal.) The successful marketer assesses the latent needs of society, creates products and services to match these needs, and persuades consumers to purchase them. The expansion of demand benefits the firm that generates it, but it also provides for growth in the economy as well.

In addition to changes in the concept of marketing's function in the business environment, modern marketing changes in response to technological developments and new business concepts. Development of the computer, television, refrigeration and the quick-freeze process, the automobile and truck, containerization, palletization, self-service, and of a host of other products and concepts markedly affects marketing activities. The spread of education and the growing influence of government in business affairs, which have accompanied growth in the United States, also influence the way in which marketing is performed. Thus, marketing functions and institutions adapt and modify themselves in myriad ways to meet the needs of the economic system.

Throughout this discussion, marketing is assumed to be an activity conducted by business firms seeking a profit. Recently, some marketing scholars question whether this is not an unnecessarily restrictive conception of marketing.[10] Kotler and Levy suggest broadening the concept of marketing to include nonbusiness enterprises as well. This broader concept recognizes that nonbusiness and business enterprises are similar in many important respects. Such nonprofit institutions as hospitals, labor unions, museums, political parties, and churches share with business enterprises a common raison d'être: "serving and satisfying human needs."[11] The fact that one institution seeks profits and the other abjures them is immaterial. Each conducts marketing activities.

What are these activities? Every organization produces a "product," each serves consumers, and each furthers its goals by using certain marketing tools. We are familiar with the products of business organizations. But nonbusiness enterprises have "products" too: ideas (Planned Parenthood, Inc.: birth control, Alcoholics Anonymous: abstention from consumption of alcohol), health care, union benefits, political candidates. Similarly each form of organization serves consumers. To varying degrees, nonbusiness organizations may also borrow the business firms' marketing tools. Whenever a nonbusiness organization adjusts its activities to meet its consumers' needs it is engaging in *product improvement*. Even though it shuns profits, the nonbusiness organization must *price* its "products" to cover its costs. Moreover, the functions of distribution (e.g., delivering health care to patients) and customer communication (e.g., making known the availability of United Fund services) can be as important to the effective functioning of nonprofit organizations as it is to firms seeking profits. Kotler and Levy argue not only that nonbusiness organizations already perform marketing functions that are similar to those carried out by business firms but also that broader recognition of the similarity and greater use of marketing techniques may improve the performance of the nonprofit sector.

Others perceive an increased role for marketing to play in advancing social issues.[12] Some social and cultural causes and activities which it is believed marketing can benefit include fund raising, health care delivery, population control, the recycling of solid wastes, urban renewal, and cultural uplift.[13] Broadening the concept of marketing to include

[10] See Philip Kotler and Sidney J. Levy, "Broadening the Concept of Marketing," *Journal of Marketing* (January 1969), pp. 10–15.

[11] Ibid., p. 15.

[12] William Lazer, "Marketing's Changing Social Relationships," *Journal of Marketing* (January 1969), pp. 3–9.

[13] Philip Kotler and Gerald Zaltman, "Social Marketing: An Approach to Planned

social issues and nonbusiness activities represents a substantial shift in focus. This extension of marketing, however, is not without its critics.[14] But in an era when attention centers increasingly on social concerns, it is understandable that attempts are made to enlarge the scope of marketing to include them. Whether this extension takes root remains to be seen.

ARE MARKETING FUNCTIONS UNIVERSAL? ☐ This discussion of marketing's adaptation to the changing requirements of a growing economy implies that the functions, institutions, and changes in both of them are universals—that is, they apply to any economic system. One might ask: How about a socialist or command system like Russia's? Aren't marketing activities associated with a profit-oriented, free market system, and therefore irrelevant in a socialist economy? A moment's reflection will indicate that socialist systems cannot avoid marketing. The functions continue irrespective of the manner in which decisions on output and resource allocation are made. A socialist economy can no more dispense with marketing activities than it can do away with production activities. Goods must still flow from producers to users, and this requires channels of distribution and such facilitating functions as storage, transportation, and financing.

The main differences in marketing emphasis between command and free market systems lie in the areas of selling, communication, and product development. In a command system, central authorities determine the kinds and amounts of goods to be produced. Objective judgment substitutes for market pressures in allocating resources to various activities. In a free market system, the consumer signals his reactions to prices and product offerings to producers who respond accordingly. Centralization of price, product offering, and production decisions in a command economy reduces the apparent need for advertising and selling. Consumers are expected to accept what producers offer them. This dispenses with the need for competitive advertising and the pressure of selling.

Social Change," *Journal of Marketing* (July 1971), pp. 3–12, and the following articles in the same issue: William A. Mindak and H. Malcolm Bybee, "Marketing's Application to Fund Raising," pp. 13–18; Gerald Zaltman and Ilan Vertinsky, "Health Service Marketing: A Suggested Model," pp. 19–27; John U. Farley and Harold J. Leavitt, "Marketing and Population Problems," pp. 28–33; and William G. Zikmund and William J. Stanton, "Recycling Solid Wastes: A Channels-of-distribution Problem," pp. 34–39.

[14] David J. Luck, "Broadening the Concept of Marketing—Too Far," *Journal of Marketing* (July 1969), pp. 53–55.

What happens when discretionary income increases enough so that consumers no longer accept what planners provide for them? We have seen this development in the Soviet Union in recent years. The result has been a modification of the rigid, centrally-directed system. A number of consumer goods plants now have greater freedom to respond to market demands. Judged by the achievement of profits, these freed-up enterprises now exercise greater authority than before over pricing, product development, and the eventual disposition of their output. The Russians use profits to evaluate performance rather than as a reward for risking capital as a free enterprise system does. Nonetheless, this new orientation demands that marketing receive greater emphasis to help in achieving profit goals.

The Yugoslavian model makes even greater use of the trappings of marketing. This system lies somewhere between a planned, socialistic state and a free market system. The state limits private ownership of capital. It establishes broad output priorities which it controls through restraints on financing, but it leaves micro-plant-level decisions on output, pricing, product characteristics, and the like to the plant managers. They, in turn, answer to Workers' Councils composed of representatives from each enterprise. The system encourages the achievement of profits that either flow to the workers as bonuses, are plowed back into the enterprise, or are invested in local endeavors that are deemed worthwhile (e.g., new schools, housing, etc.) This system lays almost as much stress on effective marketing as we find in a completely free enterprise system. Marketing research may be less sophisticated and less prevalent and advertising less persuasive than in the United States, but these conditions reflect more Yugoslavia's stage of development than its commitment to marketing.

Several things stand out, then, in this assessment of various economic systems. First is the pervasiveness of marketing's functions and institutions. Buying and selling, transporting, storage, financing, grading and standardization, and communicating must be performed in each system. Retailers, wholesalers, and other intermediaries must exist. The emphasis on various functions may differ from one system to another, but they still go on. The most notable distinction comes in the relatively lesser use of advertising in a command system because of the reduced emphasis on competition and demand creation. Second, the Yugoslavian experience demonstrates the tendency of managers to stress marketing activities when they act in their enterprises' interests, despite operating in a socialistic environment. Critics of marketing decry the apparent waste that results from giving individual enterprises greater freedom. The Yugoslavians evidently feel that the gains outweigh whatever wastes may occur.

FREEDOM TO CONSUME □ Implicit in a command economic system is substitution of the state's judgment concerning the goods to be produced for the individual's. It is argued that "to justify the acceptance of a planned economy, it must be demonstrated that the three fundamental freedoms that consumers enjoy under the present economic system will be better protected under economic planning."[15] What are these "freedoms"? First is the "freedom, within the limits of his purchasing power of getting what he wants when he wants it, in the proper quality and quantity, at the place he wants it, and for a price he is willing to pay."[16] The second freedom flows from the first. It grants the consumer freedom to dictate what the system will produce. His "votes" in the marketplace spell success or failure for products. Producers receiving these signals schedule output and allocate resources accordingly. The third freedom gives the consumer the right to decide whether to spend or save his income.

Planning, as an alternate to free choice, raises several questions:[17]

"1. Can anyone but the individual consumer judge what product or service he should prefer?

2. Can anyone other than the individual consumer decide what he or she ought to prefer best in a product?

3. Can there ever be an 'impartial' source of information about products, particularly those whose qualities are subjective?

4. Can there be any place for innovation under economic planning?

5. What deficiencies of human nature can economic planning overcome?

6. What standards of more socially desirable action can be set up under economic planning?"

These questions imply answers which insist that the consumer, not economic planners, call the shots. Defenders of a free market system

---

[15] Edward A. Duddy and David A. Revzan, *Marketing* (New York: McGraw-Hill, 1947), p. 556. Used with permission of McGraw-Hill Book Company.
[16] Ibid., pp. 556–57.
[17] Ibid., p. 556.

see consumer sovereignty as a key feature of the system. Critics attack this position, arguing that sellers and advertisers manipulate consumers so that consumers dance to their tune rather than reign supreme over the marketplace. Jerome Rothenberg makes this argument.

"Consider . . . [an] extreme case. . . . There is only one firm. It uses part of its resources to produce some output without considering consumers' tastes. Then it uses the remaining part successfully to persuade the consumers that this output is exactly what they want. Are consumers sovereign here when their tastes change accommodatingly to output . . . ?

Few would insist that the consumer in this case is sovereign in any useful sense."[18]

Rothenberg realizes that life is not always this uncomplicated. First, persuasion does not always succeed. Ad campaigns fail; consumers reject certain products regardless of the pressures on them to buy. Furthermore, competing claims may drown out one another. Finally, one asks: What would happen if we multiplied the products available in Rothenberg's simplified world from one to many thousands? Now if a portion of total resources were set aside to induce people to buy them, would consumers' tastes still accommodate to available output? Even if the answer is "yes," one might then wonder if persuasion disappeared, which goods would consumers demand that they do not now consume? We can assume that they would continue to select from the vast array available to them. In a sense they would be no more sovereign than they were when persuasion (advertising) existed. But when the effect of persuasion had worn off, consumers would be free to make unfettered choices. The extent to which they ordered new wants would measure, roughly, the distorting influence of advertising pressure. One can only speculate what goods and services people would consume without advertising. Marketing's critics may be surprised at the power of other factors such as social pressure and emulation. The international "demonstration effect," which accounts for the transnational spread of product preferences and consumption patterns, points up the power of emulation as a demand determinant. The same kind of want-generating influence undoubtedly works within an economic sys-

---

[18] Jerome Rothenberg, "Consumers' Sovereignty Revisited and the Hospitality of Freedom of Choice" in Lee E. Preston (ed.), *Social Issues in Marketing* (Glenview, Ill.: Scott Foresman, 1968), p. 265.

tem. Advertising may reinforce the process, but it is hard to imagine that it would still not function in the absence of advertising. In any event, the issue of advertising's role in want-creation cannot be resolved without banning its use completely, an unlikely event.

AFFLUENT SOCIETY THESIS ☐ The preceding discussion raises several important subissues that can be stated as questions. Does a high-level economy need demand- and want-creation to sustain economic growth? Does demand-creation lead to the distortion of priorities, with the acquisition of more material things and gadgetry winning out over the consumption of community goods? If we restrict the freedom of the consumer to decide his consumption priorities, what mechanism will replace him as a decision-maker?

John K. Galbraith's *The Affluent Society* popularized the issues. Galbraith reminds us that the law of diminishing marginal utility should result in added output diminishing in importance since the marginal utility from its consumption declines. But he sees economists finding a way around this outcome. "While the marginal utility of the individual declines in accordance with the indubitable law, the utilization or satisfaction from new and different kinds of goods does not diminish appreciably."[19] Why should economists need to modify the law of diminishing marginal utility? They need to affirm the continuing importance of production as an economic activity. Production—and ways to increase it efficiently—lies at the heart of economics. So, Galbraith implies, economists extend marginal utility theory to provide a kind of occupational insurance.

The conventional wisdom holds that goods chosen yesterday are not necessarily more important (i.e., have a higher marginal utility) than those consumed today. A person changes. Today he is different from the person he was yesterday. He has new wants and priorities. Galbraith finds it hard to imagine that later consumption is less urgent than earlier, and here he detects a flaw in the conventional position. "If the individual wants are to be urgent they must be original with himself. They cannot be urgent if they must be contrived for him."[20] This is the core of Galbraith's thesis. Also central to his argument is the assertion that "as a society becomes increasingly affluent wants are increasingly created by the process by which they are satisfied."[21] Furthermore,

---

[19] John Kenneth Galbraith, *The Affluent Society* (Boston: Houghton Mifflin, 1968), p. 148.

[20] Ibid., p. 152.

[21] Ibid., p. 158.

"it can no longer be assumed that welfare is greater at an all-round higher level of production than at a lower one. It may be the same. The higher level of production has, merely, a higher level of want creation necessitating a higher level of want satisfaction."[22] Advertising and emulation contribute to the want-creation. This phenomenon of wants depending on a "process by which they are satisfied," Galbraith labels the "Dependence Effect."[23]

Let us analyze his thesis. First is the issue of the urgency of one's wants. Galbraith fails to demonstrate that wants, to be urgent, must originate with the individual. His evidence of wants' lack of urgency is that salesmanship and advertising must be used with intensity to convince people to buy. This argument overlooks the *possibility* that consumers do not require large doses of selling and advertising to persuade them to buy new products. Much advertising tries to convince people to buy a particular brand rather than the product itself. The failure of ad messages to penetrate the "noise" in the communications process also accounts for overkill in its use. Moreover, there is more advertising than there is time available to absorb it. This is bound to lead to enormous waste.

Wasted communication is not unique to advertising. Any teacher realizes that many of his "messages" fail to get through to his students. Barriers to communication are infinite. Students may be distracted by a pretty girl walking outside the classroom window, by a professor's annoying mannerisms, by the boredom of the subject which leads to switching off the listening mechanism. The recipient of ad messages may not "hear" for similar reasons. He may also require several exposures to a message to comprehend the value of a product. Also much advertising is wasted because those exposed to it—though they may understand the message and desire the product—may be financially unable to buy it immediately.

There is also the matter of the forces that stimulate want-creation. Galbraith dismisses those that arise out of advertising and social emulation. But can wants be written off because we acquire them this way? Should we treat them differently from those derived from education, from family associations and other personal relationships and from the culture in general? Von Hayek claims that beyond innate wants of food, shelter and sex, the others "we learn to desire because we see others enjoying various things. To say that a desire is not important because

[22] Ibid.
[23] Ibid.

it is not innate is to say that the whole cultural achievement of man is not important."[24] He argues further that nearly everything we consume is influenced by our social environment. Man does not intrinsically like literature or various art forms. Production of them creates their own demand. How does this differ from the affluent wants that Galbraith sees "created by the process by which they are satisfied?"

Let us look in more detail at a fairly recent product development to determine how much utility it provides consumers. Stereophonic record players can bring quality music into an increasing number of homes. Growth in the product's demand stems from greater affluence, improved products, increasing numbers of highly educated consumers, and a good deal of promotion. For many, this product development has had a culturally uplifting impact as it has encouraged the cultivation of "good" music. Here is a case of a contrived want, one that did not exist before product development and promotion created a mass market. Does the development provide consumers only marginal satisfaction— less than they derived from products that met earlier needs? In what other ways might buyers of stereos have spent their incomes? Would alternative expenditures have increased welfare? Whose? Who shall dictate the spending priorities? If funds were to be diverted to the public support of quality music, would the cultural level be greater than with the mass consumption of stereo music and classical records? These are the kinds of questions that Galbraith's argument immediately brings to mind.

If the diminishing returns that Galbraith refers to apply to wants beyond the elementary ones, the process must begin early in man's development. Man may relieve his hunger pangs with a plate of beans, satisfy his shelter needs with a cave or crude shack, and his clothing requirements with a loincloth. Significantly, natives from primitive tribes have been found to covet trinkets and various forms of personal embellishments without the perverting influence of Madison Avenue.

Does man's desire for more goods, which advertising has stimulated, create satisfaction? If the satisfaction from their consumption did not at least equal the prices paid for them, presumably consumers would refuse to buy them. Buying them must mean that the anticipated marginal utility from the goods' consumption must be greater than the marginal loss of the money spent on their purchase. Galbraith might reply

---

[24] F. A. von Hayek, "The Non-Sequitur of the 'Dependence' Effect," in H. C. Barksdale (ed.), *Marketing in Progress* (New York: Holt, Rinehart and Winston, 1964), p. 30.

that the gain in satisfaction is adequate only because advertising has led people to believe that the goods' purchase will satisfy their wants—wants, to be sure, that advertising has created. From a hedonistic point of view, the key question may be not how the demand was created, but whether the goods did or did not increase satisfaction. If one of man's goals is to pursue happiness, and the acquisition of goods helps achieve that goal, do we quibble over the way in which demand for the goods was created?

Perhaps man fails to achieve happiness by consuming goods, the need for which was obscure before a producer created it and an advertiser convinced him to buy it. In this case he might presumably refuse to cooperate with the "system." He could do so in one of two ways. He could remain within the ambit of the "persuasive" economy but refuse to bow to it. He could tune out the "hidden persuaders' " blandishments and let his free will reign. Alternatively, he could drop out of this world and into one that deemphasizes material possessions. A significant number of people have opted for the second alternative in recent years by living in rural communes rather than being integrated into an urban society.

Because our goals have stressed spending for private consumption expenditure, Galbraith finds us ignoring public sector spending. He argues that an affluent society, with most of its members' primal needs fulfilled, should reorder its priorities. Galbraith would achieve this reordering by deemphasizing private sector spending and transferring expenditures to the public sector. Presumably, this reordering would optimize society's welfare. Whether the failure of society to embrace Galbraith's solution is attributable to advertising's undue influence, a failure of our political process, public lethargy, or a flaw in the "Affluent Society" argument itself, remains for the reader to ponder.

SATIETY OF WANTS □ Discussion of the "Dependence Effect" leads to a corollary issue. Can there exist a satiety of wants? This issue becomes important when we appreciate one of marketing's leading functions in a high-level economy. All of the traditional marketing functions discussed earlier as being performed in any kind of system continue to be performed when an economy reaches a high level of development. As indicated, the relative emphasis of some may change over time. If demand-creation is seen as part of communications, this function takes on new dimensions and added importance as economies mature. A high-level, dynamic economic system requires large and growing markets to prevent stagnation. Much of the burden of sustaining growth, therefore, falls to marketers who conceive of unmet needs, this want-creating, want-fulfilling process, however, depends upon a create satisfaction? If the satisfaction from their consumption did not continuing ability to create new wants. Hence the need to determine whether wants are subject to satiation.

How may satiety arise? Several forces could lead to it. First is the scarcity of time.[25] People's desire for goods may be infinite but the time necessary to consume them is not. The argument continues: even if time were infinite, people eventually would choose leisure over the acquisition and consumption of more goods. There are two aspects of this consideration. First, people may choose leisure over work. This refusal to work will limit the income necessary to purchase further goods. Moreover, consuming goods requires time, so a choice of leisure rules out additional consumption.

The second force leading to satiety is the belief that saturation levels exist in the acquisition of goods. This differs from the first factor although they appear to be similar. The time limitation argument says, in effect, that time forces a saturation level for *all* goods beyond which one cannot feasibly consume. The second factor points to the existence of saturation levels for individual commodities and services. This condition is said to apply both to currently consumed goods and to durables whose consumption stretches over a long period of time. Analysts of the new product development process see products exhibiting an S-shaped growth curve. They move from an introductory stage through market growth, maturity as the product approaches a saturation level and, eventually, into decline.

The saturation theory ignores several things:[26]

1. It ignores quality changes. People consume a finite, easily attained limit of food, for example, but food processors continually build convenience into their products which shifts labor output from the family kitchen to the factory kitchen.

2. Saturation rates expand as consumers acquire additional versions of the same product. Second and third cars, homes, and television sets are cases in point. A corollary of this condition is the lower utilization rate of goods when more than one is pur-

[25] For a discussion of the limiting effect of time, see Staffan Burenstam Linder, "Are We Approaching the Limit of Consumption?" in *Featuring Sweden* (#5, 1963).
[26] Ulrich Herz, "Towards the Saturation Society" in George Fisk and Donald F. Dixon (eds.), *Theories for Marketing Systems Analyses: Selected Readings* (New York: Harper & Row, 1967), pp. 181–83.

chased. This point ties in with the time limitation conditon just discussed. This expansibility of saturation rates demonstrates that although time may limit *consumption,* it may have less impact on *acquisition,* which is the key factor in a discussion of satiable wants.

3. People may elect to consume goods faster by discarding them before they wear out or by buying disposable products. Given the relatively faster increase in service costs than new durable goods costs, consumers may increasingly discard out-of-order appliances rather than repair them. Recent years have seen the introduction of a host of disposable products with no indication that the trend toward their use will lessen.

4. The saturation theory ignores the relative increase in services whose growth potential is enormous. Growth curves tend to concentrate on material goods, yet the consumption of services grows relatively faster than goods' consumption in high-level economies. Obviously, even services must reach some point of satiety or we will observe, in fact, the Chinese proverbially taking in each other's laundry.

5. Despite Galbraith's hopeful title, a large percentage of the American people live outside of an affluent society. They might consume as much as the more affluent if they possessed the necessary income. So there is plenty of room for expansion of their consumption as there is for that of middle-income families that may aspire to high income-living standards.

The time-constraint argument also has limitations. Leisure may, and usually does, involve the consumption of goods or services. Leisure and consumption are not mutually exclusive. One can even argue that increased leisure provides more opportunity for consumption than does a more work-oriented system. The argument also ignores the time-saving element involved in many goods. These goods, in effect, stretch the time available for consumption. Finally, the time-limiting argument fails to realize the nature of many consumption processes. It takes no more time to "consume" a $10 tie than it does a $5 one. There is no more consumption involved in driving a Cadillac than a Ford. One could multiply these examples manyfold. A Rockefeller has no more available time to consume than we do, yet he undoubtedly spends a good deal more on consumption than we.

If wants are not satiable in the foreseeable future, there is still room for marketing to perform its function of visualizing unmet needs, creating products to meet them, and promoting their sale. But this leaves unanswered at least two more fundamental and philosophical questions. First is the question of whether the finite supply of the world's raw materials permit us the luxury of unlimited consumption. This question used to be phrased in terms of the eventual need to face up to resource limitations. Recent ecological developments demand that we consider this problem sooner rather than later. The second question concerns the goals and purposes of man. Are people who are endowed with material possessions and work-saving devices more fulfilled and happier than those who lack modern comforts? Each reader can answer this question himself.

A final note: it is interesting that a discussion of satiety usually ignores the possibility of a limit on production capability. The limiting factor to continued growth is presumed to arise out of consumption. If one assumes zero population growth and no increase in the number of hours worked, output increases depend upon continual increases in productivity.[27] Can this process continue indefinitely? This question is no more easily answered than is the one concerning the satiety of wants. But as a growth-limiting factor, it looms as large in importance as does want-satiation. And certainly the limitation of natural resources to sustain growth is a more probable candidate than either consumption or productivity to put a ceiling on output.

□ **DISCUSSION QUESTIONS** □

1. Distinguish among the use of market exchange systems, reciprocity, and redistribution as ways to distribute goods. Who controls each of the three systems?

2. We associate prices with a market exchange system. Must prices necessarily exist in such a system? Defend your answer.

---

[27] Even if we do not postulate zero population growth, growth must cease eventually when the earth will sustain no more people. The assumptions here also call for a constant labor force size. Increasing the numbers of working women and lowering and raising the working age limits, could help sustain higher output, but even with these changes, one attains an eventual ceiling.

3. Prices exist in a market exchange system but cannot occur either under systems of reciprocity or redistribution. Agree or disagree?

4. Although the United States operates principally under a market exchange system, the commune movement relies, ideally, on reciprocity. To what extent might the trend toward commune living develop in the United States? What effect might substantial growth of this development have on the viability of the market exchange system? Can commune inhabitants divorce themselves completely from the market exchange system? Explain.

5. Distinguish between physical markets and the market mechanism.

6. Does the economizing principle portrayed in Figures 1–1 and 1–2 in this chapter settle the argument about the alleged wastes associated with retailing? Explain.

7. Set up a matrix with marketing's various functions (buying and selling, storage, financing, etc.) in the column headings and a "planned" system and "free market" system in the row headings. Indicate in each cell of the matrix whether the function is "very important," "fairly important," or "unimportant" to the effective functioning of the economic system.

8. What is consumer sovereignty?

9. Is society better or worse off when consumer sovereignty exists? Defend your position and indicate what criteria you use when answering this question.

10. "Resolved: advertising forces people to consume goods and services that they do not need." Take a pro or con position and debate the issue with a friend or classmate.

11. Define the "Dependence Effect." Make and defend a case for or against the existence of the "Dependence Effect."

12. Galbraith says that "it can no longer be assumed that welfare is greater at an all-round higher level of production than at a lower one." Try to devise a research design to test whether, in a given society, a higher level of production results in more, less, or the same total welfare.

13. Some people argue that a continued expansion of output will create intolerable ecological problems. If so, do marketers perform a social disservice by encouraging more purchases (hence more output)? Defend your position.

2

Advertising Performance

No aspect of marketing receives more criticism than does advertising. Indeed some critics of marketing seem to view advertising and marketing as synonymous.

What are the charges against advertising? First, it is wasteful. It drains off valuable resources into nonproductive activity. By raising costs it also raises prices. Advertising is manipulative. It "sweet talks" us into buying things that we do not want or, worse, that are bad for us. It creates desires where none existed before. It prods us to covet material possessions and feel cheated when denied them. Advertising adversely affects competition by raising entry barriers, making the price for admission into certain industries prohibitive to all but large corporations—and in some instances barring them as well.

These are some of the charges leveled at advertising. How close to the mark are they? This chapter examines these issues and attempts to evaluate them.

EXTENT AND GROWTH OF ADVERTISING □ Total advertising expenditures in the U.S. have grown steadily from $50 million in 1867 to $19.6 billion in 1969. Table 2–1 shows the growth of advertising in dollar amounts and as a percentage of various aggregate economic indicators. Although the totals have risen sharply over the years, advertising expenditures as a share of gross national product have remained fairly constant (aside from the World War II aberration). The percentage has increased slightly as a share of personal consumption expenditure. The difference reflects the growing share of total economic activity in the governmental sector where advertising is scarcely a factor.

Enormous disparity exists in the advertising-sales ratios for different industries and companies. In 1965, 32 of the largest advertisers spent 10% or more of their sales revenue on advertising.[1] Over half of these

---

[1] Jules Backman, *Advertising & Competition* (New York: New York University Press, 1967), pp. 14–15.

TABLE 2–1 Advertising Expenditures Total and as a Percentage of Gross National Product and Personal Consumption Expenditures, 1867–1969

Year	Ad Expenditures (Millions of Dollars)	Advertising as a Percent of	
		G.N.P.	Personal Consumption Expenditure
1867	$ 50		
1890	360		
1900	542		
1915	1,302		
1920	2,935		
1925	3,099		
1930	2,607		
1935	1,690	2.34	3.03
1940	2,088	2.09	2.95
1945	2,875	1.36	2.40
1950	5,710	2.00	2.99
1955	9,194	2.31	3.61
1960	11,932	2.37	3.67
1965	15,255	2.24	3.54
1969	19,565	2.10	3.38

Source. Jules Backman, *Advertising & Competition*, p. 182; Reavis Cox, *Distribution in a High Level Economy*, p. 103; *Statistical Abstract of the United States*, 1970.

were in the drugs and cosmetics industries. On the other hand, some industrial goods producers spend next to nothing on advertising. Table 2–2 indicates the ad-sales ratio for a wide range of industries for 1967. It includes all industries with ad-sales ratios exceeding 2% plus other representative industries. The table points up the dramatic difference in the emphasis on advertising from one industry to another. The industry at the top of the list in Table 2–2 spends 32 times the rate of the industry at the bottom.

This comparison is instructive on an important count. Much of advertising's criticism stems from the drumbeat of repetitive advertising of a few leading consumer goods industries such as toilet preparations, proprietary drugs, soap, beer, automobiles, and cigarettes. The consumer who exposes himself to various media can hardly avoid the constant pressure of importunate manufacturers to buy their products. The development of radio and television in the last few decades has accentuated the problem because of the obtrusive character of these media. Their ads are less easily ignored than are those appearing in the print

TABLE 2–2 Advertising-Sales Ratio, for Various Industries, 1967, and Contribution to Wholesale Price Index

Industry	Ad-Sales Ratio	Weights in W.P.I., Dec. 1966[c]
Costume jewelry	10.74	.237
Soap products	10.42	.436
Perfumes and toilet preparations	10.36	.437
Drugs	9.22	.888
Bottled soft drinks	6.19	.493
Chemical and allied products, not allocable	6.18	N.A.
Tobacco products	5.99	.802
Malt liquors and malt	5.89	.529
Miscellaneous food products	5.87	N.A.
Watches and clocks	4.82	.126[a]
Wines and brandy	4.38	.097
Cutlery, hand tools, and hardware	3.76	.593[a]
Toys and sporting goods	3.74	.513
Book publishing	3.50	N.A.
Grain mill products	3.37	.449[a]
Optical, ophthalmic, and medical goods	3.35	N.A.
Confectionary and related products	3.19	.099[a,b]
Canned and frozen foods	2.55	1.023[a]
Distilled liquor	2.49	.246
Photographic equipment and supplies	2.49	.386
Household appliances	2.37	.953[a]
Bakery products	2.34	1.188
Tires and tubes	2.03	.533[a]
Footwear—except rubber	1.58	
Household furniture	1.13	
Motor vehicles	1.12	
Woman's, children's, and infant's clothing	0.75	
Cotton woven fabrics	0.61	
Meat products	0.55	
Petroleum refining	0.51	
Sugar	0.37	
Total		10.028

[a] December 1962.

[b] Candy bars; solid chocolate.

[c] It might have been preferable to show Consumer Price Index weights here, but it was impossible to get data on the industry categories used for the ad-sales ratios.

Source. Internal Revenue Service, Source Book of *Statistics of Income,* 1967; U.S. Department of Labor, *Wholesale Prices & Price Indexes,* January 1967; Jules Backman, *Advertising & Competition* (New York: New York University Press, 1967), p. 208.

media. But the leading advertisers do not constitute all of industry. Far from it. Many large industrial goods firms advertise so little that many people are unaware of their existence, although they may far exceed the size of well-known consumer goods companies. The advertising they undertake may be limited to business and trade journals. Moreover, even a number of consumer goods products do not lend themselves to advertising because of their nondifferentiated character or because of the fragmented structure of the industry. Sugar and meat products are cases in point. The total value of the output of firms which, for one reason or another, rely little on advertising is substantial. Industries in 1967 for which we have data having ad-sales ratios above 2% accounted for only 10.03% of the weights in the wholesale price index.

ADVERTISING'S EFFECT ON ECONOMIC GROWTH ☐ To what extent does advertising stimulate economic growth? Here is one viewpoint: ". . . advertising, by acquainting the consumer with the values of new products, widens the markets for these products, pushes forward their acceptance by the consumer and encourages the investment and entrepreneurship necessary for innovation. Advertising, in short, holds out the promise of a greater and speedier return than would occur without such methods thus stimulating investment, growth and diversity."[2] Unfortunately, no empirical evidence exists to support this position. It lacks some substance when applied to previously mentioned, little-advertised products, many of which are industrial goods. Even in the consumer goods sector, there is the successful development and expansion of private label brands that lack advertising support. The rebuttal here undoubtedly would be that private brands cannot thrive without the development first of a demand for branded and advertised products. This problem of advertising's effect in creating primary demand for specific products is examined later in this chapter.

Jules Backman argues that the absence of advertising would reduce the incentive to create new products through research and development.[3] He points out that big advertisers, for example, firms manufacturing toilet preparations, cleaning and polishing preparations, and drugs, have witnessed sales increases proportionally greater than increases in consumer spending in general.

---

[2] David M. Blank, "Some Comments on the Role of Advertising in the American Economy" in L. George Smith (ed.), *Reflections on Progress in Marketing* (Chicago: Proceedings, American Marketing Association, 1964), p. 151. Reprinted with permission.

[3] Backman, op. cit., p. 23.

From 1935 to 1965, these three consumer groups accounted for increases in the share of personal consumption expenditures from .67% to 1.00%, from .72% to .98% and from .85% to 1.07%, respectively. During the same period consumption of these products increased from ten to twelvefold.[4] Backman claims that advertising has not merely affected market shares of various firms. "Rather it has been a significant force which contributed to an expansion in the demand for these products and to the growth of our economy with the accompanying expansion in job opportunities and in economic well-being."[5]

The question arises: What would have happened to total output in the absence of advertising? In the short run, a ban on advertising should have no appreciable impact. The carry-over effect of advertising should provide a continuing impetus to business. Buying habits should remain essentially unchanged.

The long-run impact requires some scrutiny. Take the case of an individual firm, and assume for the moment that it is able to advertise. Assume further that the company creates a new product, which it advertises, and the product sells satisfactorily. Increased sales generate increased employment as the firm hires new workers to produce the added output. Unless the new sales divert expenditures from the purchase of existing products, the increased output spells an addition to gross national product.

This conclusion presupposes that resources are available for employment. They usually are. They take two forms. First is the pool of unemployed resources that exists because the economy generally operates below capacity. This applies both to capital and labor. Even if resources are fully utilized, there is a second source. This is the "expansion" of resources that flows from increased productivity. Higher productivity means that fewer resources produce the same output, or the same resources produce more output. The process of productivity improvement "frees up" resources for new ventures. If both fail—if neither unemployed factors of production nor the capability for higher output from increased productivity is available—then the firm expands its output at the expense of others in the system. This condition results in no net expansion of total output in the system.

Now assume that the firm introduces and advertises the product but it does not sell well. What is happening here? Consumers, for one reason or another, either prefer other products to the new one or they elect to save income instead of spend it. If consumers buy alternative

[4] Ibid., p. 24.
[5] Ibid., p. 24.

products, economic growth should continue unabated. However, the election to save money should slow economic activity unless investors —government or private—put the mobilized savings to use in some productive way.

What happens now if we postulate no advertising? The new product may not get off the ground. Uninformed consumers may neglect to purchase it not because it fails to meet their needs, but because they are unaware of its existence. However, won't consumers continue to spend their income on *other* products? Does aggregate economic activity depend upon the purchase of *new* products? The production of goods and services generates incomes. Presumably individuals will spend those incomes. If this is the case, then aggregate economic activity ought to grow.

But what happens when people have consumed as much of certain goods as they could possibly enjoy or use? Consumption takes several forms. Some products are consumed continuously and almost immediately after purchase. Food is an obvious example of this kind of consumption. Other products are "consumed" over a longer period of time. Durable consumer goods fall into this category. The purchase represents only the beginning of a consumption process that may continue for years.

Each product has some effective saturation level that differs from product to product. For quarter-inch drills, it may equal, at most, one per household plus one for each professional carpenter. For automobiles, the figure may be one per person—a frightening possibility! In any event, at some point consumers will refuse to purchase more of many products, except as replacements. When this occurs, what will take up the slack? What will consumers purchase that will cause total economic activity to expand? If advertising is necessary for the successful introduction of new products, then a ban on the use of advertising may stifle economic growth since new products and services offer the outlet for expanded output.

What impact does the prohibition of advertising have on the firm and its employees? The expectation of greater sales will lead the firm developing the new product to hire additional resources. It will employ workers, build plants, and purchase materials. These decisions will generate income—latent demand—in other sectors of the economy. These are all growth-generating activities. But what happens when, or if, the new product fails to sell? Workers are laid off. Purchasing agents scale back orders for materials. Aggregate income declines, both from the loss of income of the firm's employees and from second and higher order effects that reverberate through the economic system. This is what economists refer to as a multiplier effect.

In this analysis, therefore, much depends upon the effect of the advertising prohibition on new product development. Does the development of new products depend absolutely on the use of advertising? Clearly the answer is "no." The discussion above concerned consumer products, yet industrial goods, as previously indicated, account for a great deal of economic activity. Moreover, there are other ways to push the sale of new products—personal selling and promotion of various kinds. Nonetheless, a ban on advertising would seriously hamper efforts to develop national *mass* markets for new products. Such a prohibition may re-create, to some extent, conditions that exist at an early stage of an economy's growth cycle. Less developed countries today, hobbled by low growth rates and underutilized resources, lack mass markets that permit large-scale, low-cost output. They rely heavily on local, fragmented markets. They are caught in a vicious circle of small markets and small-scale, high-cost plants. This condition prevents the establishment of low prices that will increase real income at home and expand sales abroad and bring about the necessary expansion of aggregate output and employment. Denied the opportunity to develop new products, would an advanced economy revert to an emphasis on local markets and move away from national, mass markets? Proponents of a ban on advertising need to consider the consequences of this possibility.

Is there no remedy to this problem? The Affluent Society thesis, outlined in the first chapter, may offer an alternative. Galbraith argues for a realignment of priorities to emphasize the public sector at the expense of consumer goods production. The impetus for growth would emanate from the government. Recasting priorities would involve restructuring the mix of private and public spending. Government-directed production would account for a larger share of total economic activity than it now does. People would consume relatively more in the areas of public recreation, education, and public health and relatively fewer consumer goods. Higher taxation rates would presumably drain off the increased incomes generated by the government spending. This shift of discretionary income from individuals to the government via taxation would reduce the pressure to generate growth from the private sector and would, therefore, accommodate a policy of limiting advertising.

The Russian experience seems to confirm the belief that growth can occur with minimal emphasis on advertising and other forms of sales promotion. Starting from a lower base than the United States, the Soviet Union increased its national income 205% between 1953 and 1969.[6] Most of the economy is centrally directed. The government decrees what goods will be produced and in what quantities. In the past, they emphasized the production of heavy, industrial goods. Recently, however, emphasis has shifted increasingly to the production of consumer goods.

Economic growth in the Soviet Union has occurred in the absence of much advertising. Does this indicate that the United States, too, could sharply scale down advertising without diminishing economic growth? A recent development in the Soviet Union raises doubts. The end of the Khrushchev era witnessed a gradual switch away from a command system in the consumer goods sector toward some reliance on a free market system. This shift gained impetus from the rapid build-up in inventories that occurred during the Kruschshev regime. Between 1954 and 1961, retail inventories rose from a 71- to a 94-day supply.[7] Several factors contributed to creation of a glut. Often, wholesalers dumped goods onto reluctant retailers. Inventories also piled up because of a divergence between retail and clearing prices. This was a direct outgrowth of the command system which centralized price-making authority. As discretionary incomes grew, the problem magnified itself. Consumers were increasingly able to decide whether or not to buy the goods that planners made available to them. The burgeoning total of unsold goods indicated that many consumers had decided not to buy.

The shift away from the pure command system involved implementation of the so-called Liberman plan. This plan called for decentralization of economic authority and reliance upon a modified profit-oriented system to guide economic activity at the firm level. The consumer goods firms covered by the plan still submit to central direction, but they assume greater initiative in guiding their activities. A profit system measures their performance. Emphasis shifts somewhat from the production of goods to their sale. This development and the growing production of consumer goods to match larger amounts of disposable personal income have heightened interest in advertising as a persuasive tool. Russians are now exposed to all kinds of advertising media—radio, television, handbills, and newspapers.[8] The government has created

[6] United Nations, *Statistical Yearbook,* 1970.

[7] V. Bel'chuk, "On the Relationship Between Demand and Supply of Consumer Goods in the Period of Communist Construction," *Problems of Economics,* **VII** (July 1964), p. 6.

[8] For more details on the developments discussed here, see Reed Moyer, "Mar-

state advertising agencies. Advertising expenditures are still low compared to other moderately developed countries, and little emphasis is placed on competitive advertising. Nonetheless, the Soviet Union's experience supports the view that advertising plays a key role in any system in supporting economic growth—especially as incomes and consumer goods output increases.

Those objecting to advertising may argue that we have carried the argument too far. Although critics fail to speak with a single voice, there appears to be no criticism of informational advertising. This would include such things as classified ads, the announcement of sales, and the dissemination of useful information about products, which assist customer decision making. Criticism centers on so-called persuasive advertising which, it is argued, induces people to buy one brand rather than another, may add little information to the user's store of knowledge, and may even distort product information.[9] It is difficult to imagine an outright ban on all advertising of this type but, presumably, critics would settle for a sharp reduction in persuasive advertising. The effect on economic growth, therefore, needs to be examined in light of diminished advertising rather than its complete prohibition. Whether limiting rather than prohibiting advertising would diminish the impact on new product development as discussed above cannot be answered definitively. One way to resolve this question would be to institute a limitation and observe the results. This leads to a final question: Who will bell the cat? If advertising is wasteful and is unnecessary for continued economic growth, limiting its use will benefit the economy by efficiently reallocating resources. If, on the other hand, the unimpeded use of advertising is a necessary concomitant of growth, the results of an experimental limitation of its use may be disastrous.

The impact would depend, in part, on the way in which an advertising limitation operated. A complete ban, whatever other effect it had, would give existing products an enormous edge over potential newcomers. The reduction in product differentiation resulting from a prohibition would also limit product variety. If the ban limited new product development, it would reduce the opportunities for improving the standard of living that flow from their introduction. Whether society is better off in a world with television sets, frozen foods, electrically powered appliances, penicillin, and other recent product developments goes beyond

keting in the Iron Curtain Countries," *Journal of Marketing,* **XXX** (October 1966), pp. 3–9.

[9] Although the literature often distinguishes between informational and persuasive advertising, providing clear definitions of each may be difficult.

the present discussion and is best answered by the reader. Limiting the use of advertising might well take the form of reducing the volume of competitive ads that cancel each other out. It is hard to imagine aggregate economic growth suffering from some reduction of this kind of advertising.[10] The frustrated advertiser's lament that "I'm wasting half of my advertising expenditure, but I don't know which half," supports the view that little harm would result from such a reduction.

Further support of the view that reduced advertising would not harm growth comes from an analysis of advertising-economic growth ratios in other countries. Available data indicate a tendency for total advertising expenditures to increase as aggregate economic activity increases. However, some countries maintain high growth rates with far lower levels of advertising than exist in the United States.[11]

Throughout the discussion one issue is ignored. This is the question of the social desirability of economic growth. The discussion implies that growth is desirable. In most countries of the world—especially in the less developed countries—one encounters little resistance to the goal of economic growth. However, in recent years the United States has witnessed increasing concern over the desirability of growth. The argument usually is tied to concern for the environment. Critics of unimpeded growth see increased industrial output threatening our survival through the depletion of irreplaceable natural resources and environmental pollution. Despite increasing concern over the unfavorable side effects of growth, the prevailing sentiment in the United States still appears to favor growth as a desirable goal. Whether this attitude will change remains to be seen. In a later chapter we look in more detail at some of the ecology issues as they relate to marketing.

EFFECT OF ADVERTISING ON PRIMARY DEMAND ☐ The most comprehensive study of advertising's effect on the economy is Neil H. Borden's *The Economic Effects of Advertising.*[12] Now over three decades old, it still offers analysis on the performance of advertising that is as timely as it was when originally published.

An important area of Borden's analysis is his study of advertising's

[10] We assume here that resources diverted from the advertising industry and the media that handle advertising would be reallocated to other productive activity in the economy.

[11] For supporting data, see S. Watson Dunn (ed.), *International Handbook of Advertising* (New York: McGraw-Hill, 1964), pp. 726–777.

[12] Neil H. Borden, *The Economic Effects of Advertising* (Chicago: Richard D. Irwin, 1942).

impact on primary demand. He traces the growth of several industries during the first four decades of the 20th century. His conclusions:

• **Cigarettes.** He sees advertising increasing primary demand for cigarettes by reducing prejudices against their consumption, especially by women.

• **Dentifrices.** "This period [1914–31] of increased consumption corresponded with the period of heavy increase in the use of advertising for dentifrices. Hence it seems fair to assume that advertising was an important factor in stimulating the practice of brushing teeth."[13]

• **Sheeting.** Borden finds no strong evidence showing the effect of advertising on the primary demand for sheeting. He believes, however, that advertising shifted the demand from piece goods to finished sheets and pillowcases.

• **Refrigerators.** Heavy advertising accompanied the vastly increased use of refrigerators during the 1920s and 1930s. Borden thinks that advertising and selling affect the elasticity of demand for some new products like refrigerators by gaining initial acceptance for them which, in turn, leads to emulative buying.

• **Sugar.** Borden observed a minimum amount of advertising of sugar, yet demand grew steadily, presumably from the effect of other factors.

His overall conclusion concerning advertising's effect on primary demand is cautious. Its "chief effect on primary demand has been either to speed up the expansion of a demand that naturally would have come without advertising, or to check or retard an adverse trend."[14]

Reviewing Borden's work, one is hard-pressed to find solid support for his conclusions. The growth of refrigerator sales, accompanied by increased advertising expenditures, was also accompanied by sharply lower prices. Which factor—advertising or lower prices—provided the impetus for higher sales? Or did the product's manifest advantages over the ice box plus word-of-mouth account for sales growth? How much of the growth in dentifrices resulted from advertising and how much from consumer education about oral hygiene? There is another cause and effect problem—the possibility that increased sales of a product

---

[13] Ibid., p. 296.
[14] Ibid., p. 434.

stimulate more advertising rather than vice versa. Increased usage may have encouraged more dentifrice firms to enter the industry and more to turn to advertising. In fact, between 1914 and 1921 the number of dentifrice firms advertising in leading magazines increased from 3 to 10.[15] Borden supports none of his conclusions with statistical analyses and even if he had, he probably would have encountered the cause and effect dilemmas just noted.

However, there are statistical analyses available that show advertising playing a limited role in stimulating primary demand. Multiple regression analysis seeks to uncover a relationship between a dependent variable such as automobile sales and several independent variables, for example, price and income. Researchers have conducted a number of these studies in the last several decades for nondurable and durable consumer goods, industrial goods, and agricultural products. For durables and nondurables, where advertising might have contributed to growth, the studies show that other independent variables account principally for the variation in the dependent variables. For example, using such variables as retail price, household income, scrappage rate, change from previous year's income, studies "explain" most of the variation in automobile sales, leaving little room for advertising as a determining variable.[16] Other regression studies of such products as television sets, beer, gasoline, and refrigerators reveal a similar pattern. The choice of independent variables may be different, but the explained variance is very high *in the absence* of advertising as a determining variable.

A word of caution is important here. Since regression analysis has been widely used only in recent years, most demand studies cover years when products have already matured. Television demand studies are an exception. Confined to middle and later stages in product life cycles, these regression studies fail to determine the demand determinants in the products' early years when advertising might have exerted a prominent influence.

ADVERTISING IS WASTEFUL ☐ Most of the criticism of advertising boils down to two charges: advertising manipulates the consumer and

---

[15] Ibid., p. 434.

[16] Among studies of automobile demand are those of Roos and von Szeliski, Suits and Chow, and Atkinson. The Commerce Department has also conducted demand studies for durables. For a brief review of some of this research, see Milton H. Spencer and Louis Siegelman, *Managerial Economics* (Homewood, Ill.: Richard D. Irwin, 1959), pp. 161–187.

it is wasteful. There is need to study the second charge in some detail.

Borden distinguishes two types of waste from advertising. First is the inefficiency in its use and application. The other stems from the duplication resulting from the competitive process. This is the waste that critics point to with disfavor. Advertising is seen as an unnecessary annoyance. In addition to manipulating pliable customers, it uses resources that might be utilized more productively. It is wasteful by being duplicative. Not only does it pound messages into our brain with maddening persistency but it also confuses us by presenting counterclaims for an array of competitive products that are almost identical. Why pay for an activity that warps the consumer's judgment and is of doubtful utility? The share of the retail price represented by advertising for many products is substantial. This represents waste on a grand scale. So runs the charge.

What is the defense? Borden points out that waste is not confined to advertising. Producers incur other marketing costs to attract customers. They differentiate their products, extend credit, and provide delivery service to induce the purchase of their products rather than the competitors'.[17] Furthermore, much advertising is informational. In 1965, of the $12.3 billion spent on media advertising, classified advertising accounted for $1.2 billion.[18] Other local newspaper advertising amounted to $2.4 billion. A great deal of this kind of advertising represents reporting of sales and specials, and the announcement of merchandise availability rather than persuasive advertising. Also, advertising largely supports the media that carry its messages. Fritz Machlup estimates that advertising covers 60% of the cost of operating periodicals, 70% of newspapers, and 100% of radio and television.[19] Without this financial support, consumers of the media would be required to make up the loss of revenue either by being charged more or by being taxed (if radio and TV were to become supported by the government as they are in the United Kingdom). However, from an economic point of view, direct government subsidy of radio and TV may be a more efficient way to pay for the operation of these media. But the gain in economic efficiency must be balanced against the possible loss of freedom that could accompany government sponsorship of radio and TV. Critics of the media might respond to this point by arguing that threatened government interference poses no more serious threat to freedom of ex-

[17] Ibid., p. 297.
[18] Backman, op. cit., p. 30.
[19] Ibid., p. 31.

pression than does the current commercial system which finds large corporations financing the programming.

Finally, some waste is inevitable in a competitive system. Indeed, waste and duplication are the prices an economy pays to maintain a free market system. Those who attack the waste of competition are really attacking the competitive process itself.

This is a summary of the charges of wasteful advertising and a rebuttal. To evaluate the allegation of waste requires more detailed information than we now have. The Machlup findings represent rough estimates. A better evaluation of the "wastes" of advertising requires more precise calculations. These would cover not only the cost of advertising, net such trade-offs as the financial support of media, but also the nonmedia costs of advertising. These need to be included in the total to get a true evaluation of the resources devoted to advertising. It also needs a determination of the merits of partially financing the media with advertising revenue. Could it be done more effectively some other way? Part of the media's costs now represent costs of soliciting the revenues that are used to help support the media. Perhaps this is a waste that some other form of financial support could avoid. There may be other drawbacks to the use of advertising revenue to support the media—for example, possible editorial interference. Better data would also measure more closely the content and source of advertising to determine better how much is informative and how much is persuasive. Finally, whoever evaluates the alleged waste of advertising must determine whether the maintenance of a competitive system is worth the price and whether competition can flourish with a lower level of advertising.

EFFECT ON COMPETITION □ The previous discussion concerned one important performance criterion—efficiency (but in the negative sense of measuring waste). There are other performance and conduct criteria. These include: (1) an analysis of the relation between advertising and profit rates and between advertising and concentration rates; (2) the effect of advertising on creating entry barriers; and (3) a conduct criterion, the influence of advertising on prices. These analyses should throw light on the impact of advertising on competition.

Advertising faces the charge that it diminishes competition by erecting entry barriers that small firms cannot penetrate. There are several subproblems here. First, certain products need large advertising expenditures to let them compete in national markets. The price, in annual advertising expenditures, for entering the cigarette or dentifrice market is enormous. Second, advertising expenditures benefit from economies of scale that give large firms another advantage. The scale economies arise principally from discounts that media grant to large advertisers. This gives large advertisers more exposure per dollar expended. Third, the need for large-scale advertising may increase the size of optimum-scale plants so that few firms are necessary to serve a given product market.

There are several rebuttal arguments to the entry barrier charge. Some evidence shows that the discount advantage for large advertisers may be illusory. Also the use of participation arrangements in TV advertising and regional issues of magazines increases access to these media. Jules Backman offers several other arguments.[20] He cites the market opportunities that are available in regional and local markets. Many products enjoy strong market positions in local markets in competition with national brands. The regional or local firm's small size may pose no entry barrier problem. Furthermore, advertising effectiveness may count for more than the volume of advertising. The small firm may compensate for its size with effective advertising. This, coupled with a superior product, may be enough to overcome entry barriers that massive advertising needs are supposed to create. The success of Toni, Glass Wax, and Stopette attests to the strength of small but effective advertisers in overcoming the entrenched competition of larger firms.

Backman mentions two other factors that weaken the entry barrier arguments. First, entrants need not be new firms. Diversification moves firms into new product areas. If the companies are large they can afford high advertising budgets as easily as existing producers. Thus, they are not deterred from entering by the need for massive advertising. Second, potential entry may keep competition nearly as viable as actual entry does. The threat of entry may restrain firms in the industry from engaging in anticompetitive activity.

Available data seem to support the position that high advertising requirements do not necessarily deter new market entrants. Backman cites the explosion in the number of deodorant brands (459 in 1964), cigarettes, hairspray, and dentifrices that have flooded the market in recent years. Between 1950 and 1963 the number of soap and detergent products available to grocery stores increased from 65 to 200; paper products increased from 52 to 145, baking mixes and flour from 84 to 200.[21] Backman fails to point out that more brands do not neces-

[20] Backman, op. cit., pp. 42–51, for a rebuttal of the entry barrier charge.
[21] Ibid., p. 68.

sarily spell more producers. Existing firms try to spread-eagle the market by offering new brands with an appeal to different segments of the market. Also, a few brands dominate most markets even when the industry includes many small firms.

There is another aspect to the entry barrier issue. Advertising is alleged to weaken competition by creating brand loyalties strong enough to discourage potential entrants. Brand loyalty studies find fairly sharp shifts in loyalty over time for certain classes of products.[22] A study by Lester G. Telser uncovered moderate shifts in market shares for leading firms in industries with high ad budgets. He compared market shares in 1948 and 1959 for (1) foods, (2) soaps, waxes, and polishes, and (3) toiletries and cosmetics. For the three groups, average market shares for the leading brands in 1948 declined from 42.6% to 34.1%, 38.9% to 29.9%, and 35.5% to 25.4%.[23]

Expansion in the consumption of private label brands also weakens the entry barrier argument. A survey of sales by retailers of nine product categories revealed that private label and unadvertised brands accounted for from 34.7% to 54.7% of total sales in each category.[24] The growth of private label merchandising attests to the growing opportunity in some product lines for manufacturing firms to thrive without resort to advertising. Of course, private branding is not restricted to the small firms. Many major firms which use highly advertised brands in some markets rely on private labeling to serve other markets. Small firms that must fall back on private labeling to serve markets barred to them by high advertising barriers may achieve satisfactory profits, but they weaken their chances to earn abnormally high profits which differentiation through advertising may accomplish for them.

Joe S. Bain has conducted the most searching inquiry of the barriers to entry.[25] It may be instructive to summarize his findings. He determined the impact of product differentiation on the creation of entry barriers. This goes beyond the effect of advertising alone since differentiation stems from all factors that impel buyers to select one brand rather than another. These include differences in quality and product features, buyer

[22] For example, see Ross M. Cunningham, "Brand Loyalty—What, Where, How Much?" *Harvard Business Review* (January–February 1956), pp. 116–128.

[23] Lester G. Telser, "Advertising & Competition," *Journal of Political Economy* (December 1964), p. 550.

[24] *Special Studies in Food Marketing*, Technical Study #10, National Commission on Food Marketing, June 1966, p. 20.

[25] Joe S. Bain, *Barriers to New Competition* (Cambridge: Harvard University Press, 1956).

ignorance of product attributes, and locational advantages, as well as various sales promotional activities, including advertising.

Several findings emerge from Bain's detailed study of 20 consumer and industrial goods markets.[26] "First, product differentiation is of at least the same general order of importance as an impediment to entry as are economies of large-scale production and distribution." ". . . the product-differentiation barrier to entry differs widely among industries ranging from 'slight,' through 'moderate,' to 'great.' "

"Second, great entry barriers are more frequently attributable to product differentiation than to scale economies in production and distribution. Only two of our twenty industries qualified as having such barriers on the basis of these scale economies alone—automobiles and typewriters.[27] But these two and roughly four more qualified as having great product-differentiation barriers. Extreme barriers to entry . . . seem to be linked to a substantial degree with product differentiation in favor of large established firms."

"Third, the sources of high barriers to entry attributable to product differentiation are varied and complex, but several things stand out as important. Although the simple force of heavy advertising plays a significant role in most cases, the strategic underlying considerations in strong product differentiation seem frequently to include (1) durability and complexity of the product . . . generally associated with poor consumer knowledge or ability to appraise products, and thus with dependence on 'product reputation' . . . ; (2) integration of retail dealer-service organizations by manufacturers, either through ownership or exclusive-dealing arrangements . . .; (3) importance of 'conspicuous consumption' motives on the part of purchasers, attributed mainly to the manner or surroundings in which the goods are used by the buyer." These conclusions might "suggest that advertising *per se* is not necessarily the main or most important key to the product-differentiation problem as it affects intra-industry competition and the condition of entry."

Overall, the evidence points to advertising's creating less than a complete barrier to entry—less perhaps than is commonly assumed. Whether it effectively impedes entry depends partly on the industry studied. Almost half of the products that Bain analyzed were industrial goods. Part of Backman's argument rested on the ability of existing

---

[26] Bain, ibid., pp. 142–143. Reprinted by permission of the publishers.

[27] Industries studied by Bain were flour milling, shoes, canned fruits and vegetables, cement, distilled liquors, farm machines (except tractors), tractors, petroleum refining, steel, metal containers, meat packing, rubber tires, gypsum products, rayon, soap, cigarettes, automobiles, fountain pens, copper and typewriters.

large firms to enter new product fields. But the odds are stacked against the successful entry of a small, consumer goods firm into product areas where advertising looms large in importance—especially in national markets. This condition may have pronounced anticompetitive effects on prices and profits in the affected industries and may adversely affect concentration ratios.

Why should concentration ratios be of concern? Economists point to the possible linkages between structural conditions in an industry and industry performance. An important structural factor is the number of firms accounting for a specified share of industry output. Other things being equal, a large number of firms in an industry (low concentration ratios) ought to encourage vigorous price competition and lead to normal profits. A few large firms dominating an industry might limit price competition and contribute to monopolistic profits. Thus, one needs to see whether an association exists between high concentration rates and high advertising levels.

The evidence points to such an association although it is far from conclusive. A study by Telser found a statistically insignificant ($r^2 =$ .03) correlation between the ad-sales ratios and share of total sales won by the top four firms in 42 consumer goods industries.[28] His study covered the years 1947, 1954, and 1958. A Census Bureau study showed that 13 of 50 industries had the same Big Four (four leading firms in the industry) in both 1947 and 1958. Only one of these 13 had an ad-sales ratio greater than 3%.[29]

Both of these studies suffer from limitations. The latter does not *necessarily* deal directly with concentration; rather it centers attention on the make-up of the four leading firms in each industry. Changes in the composition of industry leaders could occur without a reduction in concentration ratios. In fact, concentration could increase. The Telser study has several limitations, which Telser acknowledges. Not least of the problems is the ambiguity arising from using government data that group several product lines into "industries." Advertising propensities may differ widely for the various products included.

Contrary findings include the following:

• A study of 36 industry or product classes which made heavy use of television advertising found that four-firm concentration ratios had increased for 25 in 1963 compared with 1947 and 1954.[30]

[28] Telser, op. cit., pp. 537–562.
[29] Backman, op. cit., p. 113.
[30] John M. Blair, Statement at Hearings of Subcommittee on Antitrust & Monop-

• In 12 of 17 industries with high advertising rates, concentration increased between 1947 (or 1954) and 1963. A little over one-half of the industries with moderately differentiated products and around one-third of the undifferentiated product industries witnessed increases during the same period.[31]

• Backman, analyzing the effect of advertising rates on industry dominance by a few large firms, notes the shifting of market shares among the leaders—presumably evidence that advertising cannot necessarily prevent loss of markets. Yet in beer—one of the industries cited by Backman—the four-firm concentration level increased from 21% to 34% between 1947 and 1963.[32]

• Other research shows a "marked relationship" between advertising-sales ratios of 14 four-digit industries and concentration rates in the 1954–1963 period.[33] This appears to contradict Telser's findings and may carry more weight than Telser's research by more satisfactorily dealing with data limitations.

• Finally, C. Y. Yang found that the number of firms in industries whose ad-sales ratios increased between 1948 and 1958 declined.[34]

The scales seem to be tipped in favor of a relationship between high advertising and high concentration rates. If such a relationship is to affect performance (profits, specifically) it will do so partly from its impact on prices. Therefore, let us examine the charge that advertising leads to monopolistic prices.

Backman summarizes the argument as follows:

"1. Advertising encourages product differentiation in order to develop selling points.

oly, Committee on Judiciary in *Concentration and Divisional Reporting,* Part 5, U.S. Senate, 89th Congress, 2nd Session, 1966, pp. 1888–1910.

[31] Willard F. Mueller, Statement at Hearings of the Select Committee on Small Business, *The Status of Small Business in the American Economy,* Part 2, U.S. Senate, 90th Congress, 1st Session, pp. 447–495.

[32] Lee E. Preston, "Advertising Effects & Public Policy," mimeographed paper presented to American Marketing Association Conference, Denver, Colorado, August 28–30, 1968, p. 20.

[33] H. M. Mann, J. A. Henning, and J. W. Mecham, Jr., "Advertising & Concentration: An Empirical Investigation," *The Journal of Industrial Economics,* **XVI** (November 1967), p. 38.

[34] *Concentration and Divisional Reporting,* op. cit., pp. 2153–2163.

2. The differentiated product then pre-empts a share of the market by building up customer loyalty.

3. This makes demand less elastic, that is, less responsive to changes in price.

4. As a result, the firm is able to charge higher prices."[35]

Backman's rebuttal stresses the failure of this line of argument to consider the potentially favorable effects of scale economies resulting from advertising-induced higher sales and production. These economies may more than compensate for the advertising expenses incurred. Furthermore, if ad expenses were eliminated, firms would substitute other means of selling their products, for example, enlarging the personal selling effort. Backman further contends that factors other than costs determine prices—such factors as the degree of competition in the industry and the stage in the product's life cycle. But the level of demand, which is influenced both by these factors and by the firm's advertising expenditure levels, will influence price via its effect on costs. In other words, costs, in the final analysis, affect prices but it may be a second-order effect that depends upon demand factors.

Supporting the view that the use of advertising raises prices is the observation that advertised products tend to be more expensive than nonadvertised goods.[36] This may result from the emphasis on high quality by producers of advertised products to protect their brand image.

There appears to be little evidence of advertising's effect on prices. To learn the impact of advertising on competition, then, one might do better to measure performance directly rather than to study price behavior. The ultimate test of performance is profit. How do heavy advertisers' profits measure up to those who advertise less?

Donald F. Turner finds that industries which advertise heavily tend to have higher profit rates than low advertisers.[37] His 1954–1957 study of 41 industries reveals that industries with an advertising-sales ratio above 3% earned a 12% average return on invested capital; those spending less than 3% earned a 10.8% return. A study of the 111 largest advertisers in 1965 found their average return on invested capital slightly above that for the Fortune 500 largest industrial companies —13.6% versus 13.0%. Other similar studies of large manufacturing

---

[35] Backman, op. cit., p. 117.
[36] For several references to this phenomenon, see Telser, op. cit., p. 543.
[37] Reported in Backman, op. cit., p. 150.

companies produce similar results—modestly higher average profit rates for the major advertisers.

Because criticism focuses on advertising as an anticompetitive force much data have been presented. It is not clear, however, that this is the appropriate way to approach the problem. Product differentiation (among other things) distinguishes the economist's model of perfect competition from models of imperfect competition (e.g., monopolistic competition). Deviations from perfect competition open up opportunities for monopoly profits. Yet, product differentiation—a key contributor to imperfect competition—results from more than advertising. Product characteristics, including patented features, trademarks, locational factors and personal selling effort may account in varying degrees for a product's unique differentiation. Market conditions and management decisions may dictate what mix of differentiation-producing factors the firm will use. The cosmetics industry spends approximately 15% of its sales dollar on advertising; yet, Avon Products, Inc., a phenomenally successful cosmetics firm, stresses personal selling and spends only 2.7% of its revenue on advertising.[38] Table 2–3 throws added

TABLE 2–3 Importance of Selected Marketing Components for the Four Largest Companies, Breakfast Cereal and Cracker and Cookie Industries, 1964

	Percent of Sales	
Marketing Component	Breakfast Cereals	Crackers and Cookies
Personal selling	2.0	7.9
Advertising	14.9	2.2
Sales promotion	2.1	2.0
Marketing research	0.5	0.1
Research and development[a]	2.3	0.4
Physical distribution	5.2	11.7
Total	27.0	24.3

a Included with marketing components because the majority of expenditures are for new product development.

Source. National Commission on Food Marketing, *Studies of Organization & Competition in Grocery Manufacturing,* Technical Study #6, June 1966, p. 147.

38 Backman, ibid., p. 18.

light on the situation. The table shows widely disparate emphases on elements of the marketing mix for two similar industries that stress product differentiation.

Thus, legitimately, we should study the anticompetitive effects of product differentiation and not just of advertising. But if the advertising studies create thorny cause-and-effect problems, broadening the analysis to product differentiation magnifies the problems manyfold. One is hard-pressed to suggest a workable research design. Even in the analysis of advertising and competition, one is not certain how much advertising creates monopoly power and how much is a response to threatened loss of market position. Telser expands on this thesis.

"Increased advertising, far from signifying an obstacle to entry, is very often symptomatic of the reverse. It is the high turnover of brands and sometimes of firms that accounts for the large advertising outlays on some products. The most frequently cited example of advertising blocking entry is the cigarette industry, where advertising is intense and concentration is high. In fact, in the cigarette industry the sharpest increase in advertising as a percentage of sales occurred after the cancer alarms when many new brands were introduced."[39]

Significantly, however, the number of *firms* did not increase. A combination of the increased number of available brands and increased advertising appears to have been nothing more than the usual attempt to create a differential advantage for existing firms. The failure of new firms to enter the industry to provide the new brands (filter tips, low tar and nicotine content) induced by the cancer scare supports the view that advertising in this industry contributes to entry barriers.

ADVERTISING DISTORTS AND MANIPULATES ☐

"Critics of our society have arisen who feel that advertising has gone far beyond the status of being a neutral device for selling and has become a threat to the free, judging personality of the American citizen. Some claim, for instance, that advertisers can make the American people buy and think anything they wish. It is further asserted that advertisers can subvert the process of individual judgment and reduce the individual to the status of a pawn manipulated by the forces of mass communication."[40]

[39] Telser, op. cit., p. 556. Reprinted with permission of the publisher.
[40] John Dollard, "Fear of Advertising," in C. H. Sandage and Vernon Fryburger (eds.), *The Role of Advertising* (Homewood, Ill.: Richard D. Irwin, 1960), p. 307.

This quotation summarizes neatly one of the principal charges leveled at advertising—that it molds and manipulates the minds of individuals, inducing them to buy products that they neither need nor desire.

It is difficult to find concrete evidence to support the charge. Critics point to the repetitive character of much advertising and its increasing total volume as evidence that advertising perverts rational thought processes in a way that will benefit the advertiser. The belief that advertising manipulates minds is a subjective judgment. Interestingly, critics who level this charge tend to fear the consequences on *others*. They are presumably immune to the manipulation.[41] Defense against the charge takes at least two forms: that attempts at persuasion often fail and that advertising is not unique in its propensity to persuade. The first says that we need not fear the manipulation charge because advertising may not work; the second tells us not to worry because life is filled with embellishment, and advertising is only one among many creators of distortion.

John Dollard uses the first approach to defend against the charge of advertising's power to distort and manipulate.[42] The delusional nature of the charge is evidenced, he says, by the economists' assertion that advertising is wasteful. The waste stems from its ineffectiveness. If it is ineffective, how can it, at the same time, be manipulative?

Several pieces of evidence defuse the charge of manipulation. First is the failure of the Army's orientation program, during World War II, to increase soldiers' motivation to fight. Despite the efforts of skilled advertising specialists, the results weren't anything to write home about. An evaluation of the program found that "information was increased but basic attitudes were left relatively unaffected."[43]

Attempts by Chinese Communists to brainwash American soldiers and civilians in the 1950s also points up the limits of persuasion. When subjected to threats of death and when under complete dominance of their masters, attempts to indoctrinate the prisoners with Communist ideology apparently succeeded. However, the effect of the propaganda generally evaporated when control disappeared. Dollard asks, "How can advertising in a free society, not controlling the actual conditions of life produce the robotized personality which is feared?"[44]

Two other facts emphasize the absence of advertising's invincibility as a manipulative force. One is the failure of so many advertising

[41] One senses this, for example, in various works of J. K. Galbraith and Vance Packard, which criticize advertising.

[42] This section summarizes views of Dollard, op. cit., pp. 312–314.

[43] Ibid., p. 312.

[44] Ibid., p. 313.

campaigns. History records countless ad programs which, for any number of reasons, were colossal flops. Hence the critic's claim of waste might be appropriate, but not the charge of manipulation. Another deterrent to manipulation is the individual's skepticism and his ability to "turn off" advertising messages. Recall studies often indicate a weak ability to remember even the most basic elements of ad messages. Skepticism arises out of the consumer's continual exposure to competitive claims for products and the wariness which, for the experienced consumer, becomes an automatic response to the huckster's exaggerations.

A factor said to contribute to advertising's weakened grip on the consumer is his increased sophistication.[45] Clarence E. Eldridge sees this development reducing brand preference, which partly depends upon effective advertising. Today's better educated and more knowledgeable consumers are less inclined to "buy" advertised claims. A study by the American Association of Advertising Agencies showed that "consumers consciously react" to only 15% of the ads to which they are exposed.[46] Out of that 15%, one-third were considered objectionable.

Theodore Levitt enlists the second argument—that advertising is not alone in its use of distortion. But first he defends its use. He claims that "embellishment and distortion are among advertising's legitimate and socially desirable purposes."[47] Wrongdoing "consists only of falsification with larcenous intent."[48]

Who else distorts? The poet, for one. Poetry tries to create illusions and not necessarily accurate descriptions to influence the readers' perceptions. "Keats does not offer a truthful engineering description of his Grecian urn."[49] But what about motives? Doesn't the advertiser exhibit a base motive of earning a profit which is lower than the poet's or artist's purpose? It is true, Levitt says, that the ad man seeks to earn dollars; but Michaelangelo's purpose in painting the Sistine Chapel's ceiling was to "convert [man's] soul." The goal may be loftier but the

[45] For this view, see a report of a speech by Clarence E. Eldridge in E. B. Weiss, "Advertising's Crisis of Confidence" in David A. Aaker and George S. Day (eds.), *Consumerism: Search for the Consumer Interest* (New York: The Free Press, 1971), p. 124.

[46] Weiss, ibid., p. 125.

[47] Theodore Levitt, "Morality (?) of Advertising," *Harvard Business Review* (July 1970), pp. 84–92.

[48] Ibid., p. 85.

[49] Ibid., p. 85.

result of his "embellishment" has more impact than the advertiser's feeble effort.

Compare the distortions of advertising with religion's embellishments.

"If religion must be architectured, packaged, lyricized and musicized to attract and hold its audience . . . it is ridiculous to deny the legitimacy of more modest and similar embellishments to the world of commerce."[50]

Levitt continues: in many of his endeavors, man seeks to achieve something beyond reality. We are suffused in reality. We don't need more of it. Advertising goes outside of reality by promising us things that we do not have. The things may not measure up to the claims made for them, but this is true with many aspects of life. Life, Levitt concludes, would be pretty dull without distortion and embellishment.

Do the venal characteristics attributed to advertising date to the beginning of large-scale advertising, or do they precede it? Dollard claims that the advertising agency is a kind of "front man" absorbing the blows formerly directed at the producer-seller. "Scorn of the unctuous tradesman beaming over his woolens may have been transferred to the smiling people of Advertisingland."

Continuing:

"[in] the world of the primary or face-to-face group man showed all the traits, good and bad, that he shows now when confronted by mass communication. Suggestion was powerfully used in the face-to-face group. Gossip had its effect in controlling behavior. 'Facts' were what the community created them to be. The salesman or the huckster distorted his personality to please his customer. Artificial properties were attributed to objects by sales arguments in the direct buying situation. Status pressures influenced buying choices. Word-of-mouth artificially glamourized some objects and artificially damaged others. Shrewd, if unprofessional calculation of unconscious motives influenced the sales transaction. . . . The manias and crazes reported for simple people during the Middle Ages were not produced by advertising but by old-fashioned 'word-of-mouth.' All of the fallibility of human judgmental operations, and the accessibility of the human mind to influence, which is noticed today in the case of advertising was known in the simpler world of face-to-face relations. Advertising has not made man venal

[50] Ibid., p. 90.

and lack of it will not make him the individual judgmental machine which social philosophers wish he were."[51]

We cannot summarize all of the charges and defenses concerning the alleged ability of advertising to manipulate minds and distort the truth. The argument has raged for a long time and many people have hurled the charges, just as many advocates have risen to advertising's defense. Represented here are samples of the two positions.

As with many arguments, the truth may lie somewhere between the two extreme positions. Both critics and defenders of advertising seem to agree on one thing—that advertising engages in distortion and embellishment. The critic condemns this behavior as being injurious to the consumer. The justifier argues that distortion may take the form of exaggeration—of puffery—but the sovereignty and good sense of the consumer will not permit outright falsity of claims. The consumer can defend himself by refusing to repurchase goods that sellers misrepresent to him. Knowledge of this fact is enough to keep most advertisers honest. Furthermore, advertisers have no monopoly on the use of embellishment. Politicians thrive on it; artists of all kinds require it; storytellers depend on it to engage the listener's interest. Embellishment attracts attention. It arrests the eye and ear. That is its purpose. Is it more evil for an advertiser than others to use it? The defender of advertising says, "no"; the critic says, "yes." The matter of intent and purpose may be a key factor here. The critic sees embellishment being used for monetary gain by an advertiser; the advertiser, however, fails to see that others engaging in it have any goal other than personal gain in mind.

Whether advertising achieves its purposes may indicate whether or not it manipulates men's minds. The charge that it manipulates lacks empirical verification. It is presumed that *all* advertising expenditure can't be wasted! And if, in fact, it succeeds, the advertiser wins to himself patronage that he otherwise would have foregone.Whether he gains sales through "manipulation" or merely from persuasion is academic. The power of the ad message presumably convinces buyers to purchase a product or service. Despite disclaimers that ad campaigns and brainwashing attempts fail, continuing expenditures on advertising offer evidence that advertisers *believe* advertising can persuade. And ample evidence exists showing the impact on sales of effective advertising campaigns. So the persuasive power of some advertising probably cannot be denied.

[51] Dollard, op. cit., pp. 310–311. Reprinted with permission of the publisher.

This leaves unanswered the crucial question of the social impact of this condition. The critic argues that this manipulation (persuasion) forces the purchase of unwanted goods and the creation of "false" values. This charge was discussed briefly in Chapter 1. The criticism fails to distinguish between the effect of advertising that counterbalances the impact of competitors' advertising from that which attracts purchases of a class of products. In practice, the same advertising may accomplish both purposes; still one must distinguish intent from effect of the advertising. If advertiser A "manipulates" a consumer to buy his product rather than B's, it is hard to see how the customer suffers unless A's product is inferior or the advertising was misleading. Presumably, the Federal Trade Commission can handle the latter problem, and the consumer can handle the former through his failure to repurchase A's product. (Ignored here is the consumer's loss from having to pay for duplicative advertising, which is another issue.)

But advertising can have an effect other than the purchase of A's or B's product. It can persuade consumers to buy one class of product over another. It can make chrome-laden, power-packed, high-status automobiles more attractive than expenditures on housing, health care, education, or better nutrition. The importance of value judgments in this discussion cannot be overemphasized. To evaluate whether advertising's persuasive power has forced consumers to buy the "wrong" bundle of goods requires that one knows what is the "right" bundle. Preston argues that:

"tastes stimulated by advertising—such as tastes for alcoholic drinks, automatic dishwashers and cavity-free teeth—are not, in general, more or less admirable than tastes cultivated by family training and 'informal' social contact—such as tastes for education, racism, and sex."[52]

In the absence of advertising, what goods will consumers purchase? In the short run they will continue to buy the available array of consumer goods and services, most of which, prior to the ban, were presumably advertised to varying degrees. In the long run, one is not certain how purchases might vary and, more importantly, what forces might influence consumer behavior. One is struck by the impression that many of advertising's critics would prefer to see people consume more goods and services that are now little advertised (e.g., cultural activities) or services traditionally offered by government bodies. It is

[52] Preston, op. cit., p. 1.

not clear, however, how preferences for these goods and services would be developed in the absence of a persuasive tool like advertising. Evidence that these preferences are inherently derived is missing.

Thus the debate might benefit from more thought being given by both sides to the implications of reducing or eliminating advertising. If it manipulates minds, how will its elimination affect behavior? If it doesn't manipulate, what is it about advertising that annoys so many of those exposed to it?

There is a final aspect of this topic. Much of the debate between businessmen and critics of marketing results from their divergent perceptions of how markets should operate.[53] To the critic, competition means an emphasis on price differences. The marketer emphasizes product differentiation. To the critic, a product performs a primary function; he sees consumers' needs served by this primary function. The businessman visualizes secondary functions that products perform. He sees an expanding horizon of needs that he can fill through product differentiation. Finally, the critic sees information as data that help the consumer make rational decisions within the context of products' performing primary functions and serving uncomplicated needs. The businessman views information as messages helping him sell products that satisfy a variety of consumer needs.

Man has basic needs that he must fulfill to survive. But he also possesses psychological needs that may seem as important to him as his physical needs. The psychological needs predated the first ad man or the original critic of business. The goals of social status, ego-gratification, and the search for aesthetically satisfying experiences fall outside of man's primal needs; however, this does not diminish their importance. Much of what we call product differentiation tries to satisfy these psychological needs. It takes the form both of product features and advertising appeals. Thus, material goods often serve to satisfy nonmaterial goals. The consumer, and not the critic, might better determine whether he requires fulfillment of nonmaterial needs, and what form that fulfillment might take.

When one recognizes the variety of needs that people possess and the various ways of satisfying them, understanding advertising's functions becomes easier. It does more than communicate facts. It can project an image of the product as well. This facet of advertising may aid the advertiser by distinguishing, in the consumer's eyes, the adver-

53 Raymond A. Bauer and Stephen A. Greyser, "The Dialogue That Never Happens," reprinted in David A. Aaker and George S. Day (eds.), op. cit., pp. 59–73.

tised product from the competitors'. Furthermore, argue the defenders, advertising may also attribute characteristics to the product's user that gratify his nonmaterial needs. And this contributes to his perceived welfare. Who is to say whether the pleasure a woman feels from wearing a perfume advertised to lure men is any less intense than pleasure derived from a utilitarian pair of walking shoes. Each may get the job done. Are the walking shoes "good" because they are unadvertised and utilitarian and the perfume "bad" because it is "frivolous" and the need for it was generated by the product's advertising? It may be that the consumer is better able to answer that question than either the businessman or his critic.

PUBLIC'S ATTITUDE TOWARD ADVERTISING □ Until now this discussion has suffered from a defect common to most analyses of advertising's social impact. It assumed widespread disenchantment with advertising, and strong public pressure to limit its use. A research study published in 1968 finally substituted fact for fiction by reporting on the attitudes toward advertising of a large cross section of adult Americans.[54] Asked how they felt about advertising, 41% of the 1846 respondents gave answers that were favorable to advertising, 34% were "mixed," 14% were unfavorable, 8% were indifferent, and 3% made no response or unclassifiable answers.[55]

Summing up the study's findings, the authors concluded:

"Clearly the American public would be against the abolition of advertising or even its abolition in any medium. Overwhelmingly the public produces favorable comment more often than criticism. Not only do American readers and viewers find advertising informative to them, they also find it enjoyable. The attitude that says 'advertising is a necessary evil in our particular economic system, it serves to sell goods, but it annoys me' is not the prevailing attitude of the public. Much more common is the woman who enjoys thumbing through the dress ads in her newspaper or magazine, or the family that chuckles at the humor in the TV commercial. To eliminate advertising would be to eliminate one of the pleasures, as well as one of the guides, of the American public."[56]

[54] Raymond A. Bauer and Stephen A. Greyser, *Advertising in America; The Consumer View* (Boston: Division of Research, Graduate School of Business Administration, Harvard University, 1968).
[55] Ibid., p. 91.
[56] Ibid., p. xi. Reprinted with permission.

SUGGESTED REMEDIES □ If public policy opposed advertising, what forms might the limitation take? An outright ban is an obvious possibility. Outlawing the use of specific media for advertising or banning the advertising of specific products from certain existing media may be accomplished. In the case of cigarettes, such a ban has already been effected. In January 1971, cigarette advertising on TV and radio was outlawed. Pressure grows also to limit or eliminate highway billboard advertising. Effective January 1972, Canada prohibited all advertising and promotion of cigarettes.

Another suggestion would provide for setting dollar limits for specific product lines, firms and industries.[57] This approach opens up enormous problems of determining appropriate maxima. Moreover, it raises serious enforcement problems. This proposal also suffers a defect common to all measures that limit advertising—how to prevent shifting expenditures to other forms of promotion. Preston questions whether this drawback is important if the anticompetitive "culprit" is advertising.[58]

The most common suggestion to alleviate the alleged evils of advertising is to tax advertising expenditures. The taxing power could be used in a couple of ways. First the federal government might limit the tax deductibility of a firm's advertising expenditure. For most corporations this proposal could nearly double the effective cost of ad expenditure beyond the prescribed ceiling. A more prevalent suggestion calls for the taxation of advertising. This measure could take several forms from a flat sales tax on advertising to a tax on the ad expenditures of highly concentrated industries. Borrowing a suggestion of Donald Turner, former Assistant Attorney General in charge of the Antitrust Division, a Nader-sponsored study calls for a 100% tax on firms with excessive market power. Firms with a market share exceeding 10% would qualify if four or fewer firms controlled 40% of the market or eight or less had a 60% market share. The tax would apply to ad expenditures in excess of prescribed ad-sales ratios to be determined by the Federal Trade Commission.

The outlawing of television advertising of cigarettes allows a study of the effect of such a limitation. As this is written in late 1971, it is too early to tell what impact the ban has had on cigarette demand. But another repercussion was almost instantly noted—the shifting of expenditures to other forms of promotion and to other media. Advertising of cigarettes in magazines increased sharply in the months immediately

[57] Preston, op. cit., p. 24.
[58] Ibid., p. 25.

following the TV and radio prohibition.[59] Special promotions also stand to absorb much of money freed-up from the ban. Still, the cigarette industry estimates that it will spend only one-third of the $220 million it formerly laid out for television advertising.[60]

Spending freed-up advertising expenditures on other forms of promotion or on increased personal selling is only one of the drawbacks to a ban or tax on advertising. Another is the possible harmful effects on competition. Some feel that limiting advertising might benefit the large firm which might be better able than a small company to substitute effective personal selling for advertising.[61] For the small firm, competing with a large rival possessing a superior sales force and distribution system, the best hope for survival may be an effective advertising program. Limiting advertising would weaken its hand and reduce, not strengthen, competition. Also, as noted earlier in the chapter, curtailing advertising would increase entry barriers by strengthening established brands against the incursion of many new brands whose success depends a great deal on introductory advertising.

□ DISCUSSION QUESTIONS □

1. Think of a product that has been successfully introduced in the past several years. If advertising had been banned, would the product have sold as well as it has? Support your position.

2. Do you favor banning or limiting advertising expenditures? If so, would your ban or limitation apply to new products as well? What effect would a ban have on competition?

3. Draft—in laymen's terms—a bill that would outlaw or limit advertising. Be as specific as possible.

4. Can one distinguish between informational and persuasive advertising? Explain.

[59] John D. Morris, "Cigarette Ads Found Doubled in 14 Magazines," *New York Times,* May 17, 1971, p. 19.

[60] "Now That TV Has Given Up Smoking," *New York Times,* January 3, 1971, p. E-3.

[61] Bauer and Greyser, *Advertising in America; The Consumer View,* p. 375, and Preston, op. cit.

5. Is advertising "wasteful"? If so, is *all* of it wasted or just some of it? If some, which is and which isn't? What criteria of waste do you use? What does it waste?

6. Would limiting advertising affect the standard of living? How about total employment? If so, try to trace the mechanisms bringing about changes. Analyze both the short and long run effects, if any.

7. Some observers claim that the United States is more accurately described as a mixed economy rather than a pure free enterprise economy. Do you see evidence of this condition? Where? Would you expect a mixed economy to rely less on marketing than a completely free enterprise system? Explain.

8. Write down your estimate of the total advertising expenditures in the United States in 1969 using the following media: magazines, newspapers, television, radio, direct mail, outdoor billboards and miscellaneous. Compare your estimate with the statistics on these expenditures in *Printers' Ink, Guide to Marketing for 1969.*

9. Some critics of advertising argue that it should be limited "to protect people from themselves." This is especially said to apply to less well-educated people. Evaluate this argument.

10. Advertising is often criticized as a waste of a capitalistic system. How do we then account for advertising's increasing use in Russia?

3

Marketing Efficiency

How well is marketing performed? Any assessment of marketing must evaluate its performance from several standpoints. An important evaluation concerns the cost of performing the myriad activities involved in marketing. More important is evaluating the relationship between marketing inputs and outputs. A number of years ago, an influential book asked in its title: *Does Distribution Cost Too Much?*[1] This question is important but so are other questions. What should be measured, and how does one make the measurements? What are the forces leading to larger or smaller marketing costs? What has been the effect of transferring marketing functions among producers, retailers, and consumers? What are the macroeconomic effects of a reduction in marketing costs? Are there "too many" retailers? To what extent can we eliminate the "wastes" of competition and what repercussions might follow their elimination? These important macro issues begin the chapter.

HOW TO MEASURE PRODUCTIVITY □ Efficiency studies pose two problems: what to measure and how to measure it. Marketing productivity concerns itself with more than the resources used in the distribution sector. Of interest is the *ratio* of output (however computed) to inputs used in achieving the output. Productivity improves when marginal physical output increases relatively more than inputs increase, or decreases less than the reduction in inputs. It is the *relation* between the two that has meaning here.

The foregoing measures physical productivity, or what the economists refer to as technical efficiency. Economic efficiency is another way to characterize productivity. Joel Dean describes it as "an index of the ability of a process, an activity, a firm or an entire economic system to maximize the output of 'utility' or human satisfactions from

---

[1] Phrased this way, the question is bound to elicit an answer similar to the one in the following exchange: Q.: "How's your wife?" A.: "Compared to what?"

all available inputs."[2] Dean argues that marketers should rely on economic efficiency in assessing the social usefulness of the individual firm. He claims that "increasing the marketing efficiency of individual firms is the only way to improve the marketing efficiency of the entire system."[3] The efficiency of each firm would be measured by its profitability.

This concept runs headlong into what Furuhashi and McCarthy call the micro-macro conflict.[4] What is optimum for the firm may be less than optimum for society. Take the case of a firm that carves out a protected (monopoly-like) position through effective advertising. The result would probably be abnormally high profits. This would reflect an economically efficient condition according to Dean's criterion, but does society benefit? Does this really represent an efficient allocation of resources? The effective advertising probably permits prices that exceed those prevailing in a freely competitive market, to the detriment of the consumer. Economists have shown, by analysis that need not detain us, that these elevated prices result in a misallocation of resources for the economy at large.

Measuring the output of marketing is difficult. The problem stems partly from the intangible nature of marketing activities. Productivity in manufacturing is concerned with measuring either the physical volume or dollar value of the output of physical entities. The output of a steel mill will be a given tonnage of, say, cold rolled bars or plates. Expressed in dollars the output will equal the value added by production, that is, the difference between the total value of output at the mill door less the cost of material and labor inputs.

In marketing, some measurements are similar to those used in calculating productivity in manufacturing. Man-hours worked may measure the labor input in a department store or a warehousing operation. The value or volume of goods moved through the warehouse and the value added by the department store (difference between cost of goods to the store and its net receipts, i.e., gross margins) may accurately reflect output. Deriving ratios of outputs to inputs in these cases, as measures of productivity, should create little problem.

---

[2] Joel Dean, "Marketing Productivity and Profitability," *Productivity Measurement Review* (1960), p. 47. Dean's concept of economic efficiency differs slightly from the traditional definition which emphasizes the achievement of the highest dollar value of output for a given dollar value of inputs.

[3] Ibid., p. 47.

[4] Y. Hugh Furuhashi and E. Jerome McCarthy, *Social Issues of Marketing in the American Economy* (Columbus, Ohio: Grid, 1971), p. 8.

But there *are* problems. One arises from the changing character of marketing output. If the real value added by retail stores increases over time (adjusted for changes in price and total volume levels), does this really represent increasing distribution efficiency? If the quantity of labor inputs rises more than the increased value added, efficiency presumably declines. But doesn't this conclusion presuppose that a given gross retail margin covers a fixed, measurable quantity of marketing services? The stores' marketing output is reflected not in their gross margins (value added) but in the functions that they perform. In our example the functions performed may have increased which, in turn, resulted in increased value added. In this light, efficiency may or may not have decreased. There is really no effective way to determine which is the case without finding a way to quantify the functions performed. In most cases, this cannot be done. Hence, any productivity study in marketing must be viewed with caution.

The changing mix of functions performed is only one factor confounding attempts to measure productivity. These changes may result either from switches in consumers' tastes or from transfers of marketing functions from one entity to another in the producer-marketing intermediary-consumer chain. Confounding measurement are the intangible character of many marketing activities and the complex interrelationships among marketing inputs. For example, advertising may be ineffective if product development falters. Again, the fruits of advertising and selling expenditures are optimized when the two are mixed in appropriate proportions. One can measure the output of marketing in relation to its *total* inputs, but separating the effects of each input element becomes difficult, often impossible. Another complication arises out of the interrelationships between marketing and production. Marketing research expenditures may increase factory efficiency by improving production planning but they do so by raising marketing costs. Which element in the system—marketing or production—deserves credit for the improved efficiency in this case? And what is the *net* gain? Macro marketing cost studies ignore questions of this sort because they are incapable of handling them satisfactorily.

RESULTS OF MACRO MARKETING COST STUDIES □ Macro marketing cost studies fall into several categories. First are those that calculate the total value (or gross margins) added by distribution activities. Here the analyst looks at the total contribution of distribution to the economic system and perhaps compares it with the outputs of the manufacturing and agricultural sectors. Productivity ratios are ignored.

The second class of studies derives measures of marketing productivity over time for retail and wholesale institutions. This research determines the increase in distribution productivity, calculated as the ratio of output to some form of labor input. Other studies look at productivity in specific industries. Before reviewing the published results of macro distribution cost studies, let us examine what forces determine the share of our total economic activity devoted to distribution.

In a primitive economic system, activity centers on agriculture and handicraft industries. As the system develops, specialization grows. Farmers and manufacturers who previously had both produced and sold their output now depend on selling intermediaries to dispose of it. Thus, distribution as an identifiable function absorbs increasing quantities of resources and accounts for a larger share of total output. Furthermore, the shift of population from rural to urban areas reduces autoconsumption and increases the burden on the distribution sector to supply food to the population.

Other factors contribute to the growth of distribution costs. Marketing agencies perform additional services, for example, the granting of consumer credit, financing of retail inventories, and the performance of marketing research. The development of local and regional production centers coupled with the growth of national distribution increases transportation costs. The tendency toward decentralization, encouraged by President Roosevelt in the 1930s and intensified in the post-World War II period, has probably modified this tendency in the United States and, perhaps, reduced some transportation costs. Increased population density affects distribution costs in two opposed ways. Economies from agglomeration reduce some costs but increase others as a result of congestion, for instance, higher rents and terminal costs. Higher distribution costs also result from a tendency to sell in small, packaged units rather than in bulk, from improvements in refrigeration which permit the long-distance shipment of perishables, and from increased selling and advertising activity designed to induce consumption.

The factors indicated above have been at work for varying periods of time in our economic history. Some were dominant forces early in our development; others are of more recent origin. The net effect of the growth of distribution activity undoubtedly has been to increase the role of distribution in the system. Expressed as a percentage of total economic output, however, the data show that distribution's share has remained fairly constant in recent decades.

GROSS MARGIN STUDIES   The first comprehensive study of the cost to society of distribution was the Twentieth Century Fund's *Does Distribution Cost Too Much?*[5] which analyzed distribution costs for 1929. In that year, out of a total value of finished goods sold to final consumers of $65.6 billion, $38.5 billion, or 59% was represented by distribution costs. A later study noted an arithmetic error in the calculations, and this correction reduced the figure to 51.1%.[6]

Using gross margins as a measure of the cost of distribution, Converse, Huegy, and Mitchell calculated that for 1948 distribution costs accounted for 48.1% of what ultimate buyers paid for goods.[7] Converse calculated the share devoted to distribution in 1929 to be 49.2% and in 1939, 50.5%.[8] Reavis Cox, using Converse's methods for figuring distribution's share, carried the research forward to 1954 and 1958 when the figures were 45.3% and 46.3%, respectively.[9] Thus, in the last several decades, distribution has accounted for roughly the same share of the consumer's dollar. Data indicating the percent of national income originating in trade industries support this conclusion: in 1929, 15.2% of U.S. national income originated in trade industries; this compares with 16.2% in 1963.[10]

The value of distribution activities as a percent of total final purchases of goods and services varies somewhat depending on what one is measuring. Table 3–1 summarizes data for 1947, the year covered by Cox's comprehensive study of distribution costs. Value added by distribution industries for manufactured goods bought by household purchasers was higher than for all final purchases. Distribution accounted for 31.2¢ of each dollar of household buyers' purchases. More striking is the range of contributions of value added by distribution industries for various manufacturing industry categories. Total distribution costs as a percent of final purchase price ran from 22.1% for printing and publishing to 40.5% for primary metal products.

The components of total distribution costs had equally wide ranges for the 18 industries studied. The percent of total purchases accounted for by wholesale institutions ranged from 3.8 to 15.2% (average, 6.6%);

[5] Paul W. Stewart and J. Frederic Dewhurst, *Does Distribution Cost Too Much?* (New York: The Twentieth Century Fund, 1939).

[6] Reported in Reavis Cox, *Distribution in a High Level Economy* (Englewood Cliffs, N.J.: Prentice-Hall, 1965), p. 148.

[7] P. D. Converse, H. W. Huegy, and R. V. Mitchell, *The Elements of Marketing,* 5th ed. (Englewood Cliffs, N.J.: Prentice-Hall, 1952).

[8] Cox, op. cit., p. 158.

[9] Ibid., p. 158.

[10] Ibid., p. 153.

TABLE 3-1 Value Added by Distribution and Nondistribution Industries, 1947 (Millions)

| Market Value Added by: | Market Value Added to All Final Purchases from: | | | | | |
| | All Industries | | Goods Industries | | Service Industries | |
	Amount	%	Amount	%	Amount	%
Nondistribution industries	$178.0	79.3	$106.5	72.0	$71.5	93.2
Distribution industries	46.6	20.7	41.4	28.0	5.2	6.8
Total	$224.6	100.0	$147.9	100.0	$76.7	100.0

Source. Reavis Cox, *Distribution in a High Level Economy*, p. 124.

for retail institutions the range was 13.1 to 26.1% (average, 18.1%); for transportation, 2.4 to 10.2% (average, 4.6%); for advertising, 0.7 to 5.0% (average, 1.7%). Only for warehousing and storage were the percentage figures for each industry fairly uniform, generally about 0.1 to 0.2% of the final purchase price.

The range of these figures indicates something that an all-industry average tends to hide: the diversity of marketing activities in various industries. A number of factors affect the total distribution bill for each industry as well as the costs involved with each component. Some of the determinants include the weight and bulk of the commodity, its value, whether it is a consumer or an industrial good, the importance of direct selling in the total selling effort, the complexity of the product, service required for the product, structure of the producing industry, and frequency of purchase. The diversity of conditions facing different industries means that one cannot legitimately condemn (or praise) an industry for achieving a given level of distribution costs without analyzing the industry's underlying structural forces as well as the characteristics of its products.

A glance at Table 3-1 reveals that the percentages of value added by distribution are less than those indicated by the various studies referred to above. This condition calls for an explanation. Macro measures of distribution costs vary depending not only on the year analyzed but also on the industry coverage and on the comprehensiveness of the marketing costs measured. For example, Table 3-1 covers only the value added by distribution industries. How about the marketing costs incurred by manufacturers, farmers, and others who engage in marketing activities but who are not classified as distribution industries? Table 3–2 examines these activities and gives a better picture of *total* marketing costs irrespective of origin. Note that coverage is limited to the purchase of goods sold to household purchasers and excludes nonhousehold buyers, as well as the output of public utilities and services, thereby restricting the analysis to physical goods.

TABLE 3–2 Value Added by Distribution and Nondistribution Activities in Supplying Households, 1947 (Millions)

		Market Value Added by:	
	Total	Nondistribution Activities	Distribution Activities
Nondistribution industries	$58,546	$48,323	$10,223
Distribution industries	29,783	—	29,783
Total	$88,329	$48,323	$40,006

Source. Reavis Cox, *Distribution in a High Level Economy,* p. 145.

The significant feature of Table 3–2 is the breakdown of distribution costs between distribution and nondistribution industries. Adding in costs of distribution incurred by nondistribution industries raises the total by about one-third.

Considered so far are measures of distribution costs covering recent decades. Harold Barger traces the data for the United States back to 1869.[11] His summary statistics calculate two things: the proportion of the working force in distribution (retailing and wholesaling institutions) and the value added by distribution of all goods that were marketed through retail institutions.

Table 3–3 summarizes the first of these two time series. It indicates a continuous growth in the relative share of total employment represented by workers in retailing and wholesaling. The correspondence between the growth in these figures and growth of the economy, as measured by deflated Gross National Product, is striking. A regression of per capita G.N.P. (in constant 1929 dollars) on the percent of the labor force engaged in distribution for the 80-year period found a 1.13 percentage point increase for each $100 increase in constant dollar per capita G.N.P.[12] A parallel study of growth in employment in the

[11] Harold Barger, *Distribution's Place in the American Economy* (Princeton, N.J.: Princeton University Press, 1955).

[12] Reed Moyer, "Trade and Economic Progress," *Journal of Business* (July 1967), p. 272. The correlation coefficient is .968.

TABLE 3–3 Percent of Labor Force Engaged in Distribution, 1870–1950

	1870	1880	1890	1900	1910	1920	1930	1940	1950
Percent of labor force engaged in distribution	6.1	6.7	7.7	8.6	9.3	9.9	12.9	14.4	16.4

Source. Harold Barger, *Distribution's Place in the American Economy,* p. 8, with permission.

United Kingdom for 1861–1951 uncovered a similar pattern. There, an increase of £10 in real net national income per capita was associated with a 1.63 percentage point increase in the share of the labor force engaged, in this case, in commerce and finance.[13] Translating the value of the pound into dollars at an appropriate exchange rate reveals a more rapid growth of the labor force in distribution in the United Kingdom than in the United States. This would indicate relatively greater productivity growth in the United States. Later in this chapter data are given to support this conjecture.

Useful as Barger's figures are, they are subject to criticism on several counts.[14] First, he studies only employees engaged in retailing and wholesaling institutions and fails to enumerate those working in advertising, warehousing, industrial selling, and so on, who are also engaged in marketing activities. Moreover, his data include the total number of workers employed and not total man-hours, which would give a more accurate measure of employment activity in distribution. The average number of hours worked per week has declined faster in distribution industries than it has in manufacturing over the past century.[15] Finally, there is some question about the overall significance of any figures of this sort. The same objection applies to data on the percent of the consumer's dollar represented by value added in marketing. Taken alone it reveals little about efficiency in this sector; rather it indicates where a country is allocating its resources. There may be misallocations involved, but the raw data—either percent of labor force in distribution or value added by marketing—do not reveal them.

Despite the latter objection one ought to look at Barger's data on

[13] Ibid., p. 272. Here $r = .798$. Using a curvilinear function, r increases to .915, supporting the intuitive belief that the percent of the labor force in distribution ought to taper off in time.

[14] See, for example, Cox, op. cit., summarized here.

[15] Cox, op. cit., p. 155.

gross margins added by distribution agencies to take advantage of his long perspective on the figures.[16] The period covered is practically the same as with the labor force data—1869–1948. Again he includes only retailers and wholesalers.

TABLE 3–4 Gross Margins, as Percent of Retail Value for Goods Marketed Through Retailers, 1869–1948[a]

Gross Margins Added by:	1869	1879	1889	1899	1909	1919	1929	1939	1948
Wholesalers	9.5	9.6	9.6	9.2	8.9	8.5	8.0	7.6	7.7
Retailers	23.2	24.1	25.1	26.2	27.6	28.0	28.6	29.7	29.7
Total	32.7	33.7	34.7	35.4	36.5	36.5	36.6	37.3	37.4

a Barger has two series, one for 1869–1929, the other for 1929–48. Figures for 1929 were almost identical in the two series. This table uses the 1869–1919 data from the first of Barger's series and the complete 1929–1948 series.
Source. Harold Barger, *Distribution's Place in the American Economy Since 1869,* p. 57 and p. 60, with permission.

Table 3–4 summarizes his results. Although there was a modest increase in margins absorbed by distribution institutions in the early years covered by the study, the figures have remained fairly uniform during the 20th century. The stability in the most recent decades covered by the Barger study supports the findings which have already been reported. There is evidence that Barger's figures for retailer margins fail to account adequately for improved productivity resulting from the development of chains, supermarkets, cooperative wholesalers, and voluntary chains in recent decades.[17] With these adjustments, it is likely that the total gross margins have, in fact, fallen since World War I.

MARKETING PRODUCTIVITY STUDIES Thus, the first category of

[16] Barger does not distinguish between what he refers to as "gross spread" and value added. His gross spread, or margin, is "the difference between the value of commodities leaving the distribution system and their value when they entered the system." (Barger, op. cit., p. 55). This measure includes as output activities that go beyond value added by distributors (e.g., rent, utilities), hence exceeds value-added measures. This is indicative of the kind of problem facing one who tries to determine total distribution "costs."
[17] Cox, op. cit., p. 158.

macro marketing cost studies calculates the total employment in distribution or value (or gross margin) added by distribution activities. These studies indicate the magnitude of marketing activities in the total economic system, as well as their growth. However, they skirt the issue of productivity, which commands the interest of those who want to assess marketing's social role.

Again Barger provides us with the longest perspective on marketing productivity. He finds that output per man-hour in retail and wholesale distribution increased at a mean annual rate of 1.0% between 1869 and 1949, compared with 2.6% for the commodity-producing sectors.[18] More recent data support the Barger findings. In a study covering 1929 to 1961, Fuchs shows that the annual increase in output per man-hour for wholesale and retail trade trailed that of the goods sector by approximately 1.3%.[19] Table 3–5 summarizes both the Barger and Fuchs data.

TABLE 3–5 Average Annual Increases in Output Per Man-Hour, Trade and Goods Sectors, 1869–1961 (Percent)

Barger	Mean Annual Rate of Change		
	1869–1909	1909–1949	1869–1949
Output per man-hour:			
Commodity production	1.9	3.0	2.6
Wholesale and retail trade	1.1	0.9	1.0

Fuchs[a]	Mean Annual Rate of Change		
	1929–1947	1947–1961	1929–1961
Output per man-hour:			
Goods production	2.50	3.50	2.95
Wholesale and retail trade	1.69	1.65	1.67

a My calculations are derived from raw data in the appendix to Fuchs.

Sources. Harold Barger, *Distribution's Place in the American Economy Since 1869*, p. 39; Victor R. Fuchs, *Productivity Trends in the Goods and Service Sectors, 1929–61*, pp. 44–45.

One should not read much significance into the higher growth rates in productivity in the more recent years. Fuchs' data are in constant dollar

18 Barger, op. cit., p. 39.
19 Victor R. Fuchs, *Productivity Trends in the Goods and Service Sectors, 1929–61* (New York: National Bureau of Economic Research, 1964), pp. 44–45.

terms; Barger's are not. Any data-gathering job of the magnitude of these two studies and covering such long periods of time is bound to lead to different results that are not easily reconciled. Preston details some additional problems that call for caution in interpreting such productivity data. In addition to noting that the trade data exclude large segments of marketing activity that occur outside of wholesaling and retailing, he states:

". . . there is considerable conceptual difficulty in measuring the value of marketing output. For example, an increase in customer service or in the variety of merchandise available may, indeed, result in increases in both the cost and the value of marketing activity; however, price increases due to monopolistic practices or mutually offsetting competitive expenditures may not. Further, there may have been substantial increases in marketing services, such as convenience, that may not have involved rising costs or prices and are not, therefore, measured by the usual statistical procedures. Finally, there are very great differences in the measured rates of productivity change even within rather similar types of marketing activity,"[20]

for example, from one service and retail trade to another.

How do we account for the lag in productivity in marketing compared with the manufacturing and agricultural sectors? The 1% annual productivity growth rate in marketing indicates that some progress occurred. The development of self-service in food stores undoubtedly increased efficiency, as did scale economies resulting from the growth of chains. The average increase in the size of certain kinds of stores has led to efficiency gains. Harwell reports that sales per man-hour in supermarket checkout departments vary directly with the average order size.[21] Increasing the order size 10% when the order is valued at $2 increases sales per man-hour 7%. Other studies report similar evidence of scale economies in retailing.[22] Such minor technological developments as the cash register, dating back to the 19th century, computing scales (introduced circa 1900), palletization and, more

[20] Lee E. Preston, *Markets and Marketing: An Orientation* (Glenview, Illinois: Scott, Foresman and Company, 1970), p. 27. Reprinted with permission.

[21] Reported in David Schwartzman, "Productivity Growth in Food Retailing," in James Heskett (ed.), *Productivity in Marketing* (Columbus, Ohio: College of Commerce and Administration, Ohio State University, 1965), p. 34.

[22] Schwartzman (ibid., p. 34) reports on research by Eric C. Oesterle which shows payroll costs in meat departments falling from 13.2 to 8.7% of total expenses when sales per week increase from $3000 to $20,000.

recently, computers and telecommunication devices have helped to improve efficiency. But there have been few technical developments in distribution that compare with innovations in most progressive manufacturing industries in their ability to improve efficiency.

Other forces have deterred the growth of productivity in marketing. Government intervention has often tended to discourage productivity gains in retailing. The small, independent retailer has effectively lobbied for such protective legislation as minimum markup laws, chain store taxes, fair-trade laws, and the Robinson-Patman Act. These measures protect retailers from their competitors and help to perpetuate a system composed of small, fragmented merchants. Other factors than government intervention lead to atomistic competition in retailing, including the perennial urge of individuals to be their own boss and the ease of entry into the industry. These forces contribute to a retail structure that is top-heavy with small merchants whose output per store employee lags behind that of larger stores.

Statistical studies of productivity in the distributive trades reveal that sales per employee increase with increasing store size, at least up to a point. For 1958 sales per employee in food stores increased steadily from $19,200 for stores with no paid employees to $44,900 for stores with 20 to 99 employees. For stores with 100 or more employees, the figure fell to $31,400.[23] The same tendency toward higher sales per employee occurs over time, probably resulting primarily from increasing store size. In 1929 sales per worker in grocery stores totaled $9373; in 1963 the figure had risen to $23,128 expressed in constant dollar terms.[24] There are also scale economies in wholesaling. The average operating expense ratio for merchant wholesalers in 1968 with annual sales less than $100,000 was 24.7%; the ratio drops almost linearly with size to 7.3% for firms with over $20 million annual sales.[25]

INDUSTRY STUDIES As indicated earlier, a third class of macro productivity studies exists—those covering single industries rather than the entire distribution system. The preceding examples covering grocery stores are cases in point. Studies of distribution costs and productivity changes in different trade sectors reveal enormous variety. Calculations such as Barger's that output per man-hour in distribution has increased

[23] Schwartzman, op. cit., p. 36.

[24] National Commission on Food Marketing, *Organization and Competition in Food Retailing,* Technical Study #7, June 1966, p. 15.

[25] U.S. Census of Business: 1967, *Wholesale Trade-Subject Reports,* Vol. II.

1% annually hide varying performances in individual trades. Table 3–6 indicates this variety.

TABLE 3–6 Average Annual Percentage Rates of Change, Output per Man and Related Variables for 10 Selected Retail Trades, 1939–1963

Industry	Real Output per Man	Real Output	Compensation per Man
Apparel stores	0.99	1.87	4.17
Automobile dealers	2.09	4.82	5.19
Drug stores	2.68	4.71	5.29
Eating and drinking places	−0.18	2.30	5.31
Food stores	2.44	3.62	5.32
Furniture and appliances	2.88	5.37	4.88
Gasoline stations	3.25	5.25	5.08
General merchandise	1.40	3.53	4.38
Lumber dealers	1.21	3.07	4.99
Other	2.09	4.11	4.63
Total	1.63	3.67	4.90

Source. Victor R. Fuchs and Jean Alexander Wilburn, *Productivity Differences Within the Service Sector*, pp. 15–16, with permission.

One finds annual changes in output per man for various retail trades running from −0.18% for eating and drinking places to 3.25% for gasoline stations. Compensation per man increased more uniformly for the ten retail trades, suggesting that changes in labor costs per unit of output varied substantially among the trades.

The table also indicates a strong correlation between increases in total output and in output per man for the ten retail trades.[26] Preston has noted the same relationship and ponders its possible significance:

"We cannot, of course, easily infer the causal mechanism that is involved here. Do the activities grow because they become more productive or do they become more productive because they grow; or are both growth and productivity improvement the results of some other, as yet unidentified, phenomenon?

"These questions are not solely of intellectual interest; their answers suggest important implications for marketing management. In an econ-

[26] Rank correlation coefficient = .91, significant at .01 level.

omy characterized by rapid technological progress and increasing labor productivity, are less progressive activities doomed to extinction? If so, the critical managerial task is to develop new and more productive marketing technology. On the other hand, if rapid growth in total output is the key to productivity increase, then increasing demand is the principal task, and cost reductions may be expected to follow rather directly. . . . is it possible that the demand for marketing services is so inelastic that the sector will continue to grow, in spite of rising costs, relative to other sectors of the economy? Some portions of marketing activity seem to fit each of these descriptions, and thus the critical challenge for marketing management differs substantially from one area and industry to another.''[27]

INTERNATIONAL COMPARISONS OF MARKETING PRODUCTIVITY

☐ A comparative analysis of marketing productivity in different countries may promote understanding of some of the forces determining marketing efficiency. Figure 3–1 shows the relationship between private consumption expenditures per capita and sales per person in retailing in 1955 for 18 countries. The line of fit is fairly good; $r = .76$. One can make a good case for excluding Finland, Iceland, and Norway, the three countries with unusually high sales per retail sales employee compared with their private consumption per capita.[28] When these countries are excluded, the correlation coefficient increases to .84.

If sales per person engaged in retailing is a rough indicator of improvement in trade efficiency, then Figure 3–1 shows an association, at least, between growth in efficiency and growth of per capita consumption. Whether there is a causal relationship and, if so, the form it takes is a matter of conjecture. It is likely that the relationship between increased efficiency and its determinants is more indirect than Figure 3–1 might indicate. Unfortunately, there are no hard data to allow more positive statements.

Consumption patterns undoubtedly affect trade efficiency levels. Higher per capita personal consumption figures correspond with a relative transfer of consumer expenditures from food purchases, which

[27] Preston, *Markets and Marketing: An Orientation*, p. 27 and p. 29. Reprinted with permission.

[28] Several factors contribute to the relatively high retail sales/employee figures: Norway's high sales tax, inclusion of some wholesale sales in Norway's retail sales figures, Iceland's doubtful trade figures, the near-monopoly position of consumer co-ops in many regions of Iceland and Finland which increases average store size, and, a related factor, the existence of fewer retail stores per capita in Ireland and Finland than in other countries studied.

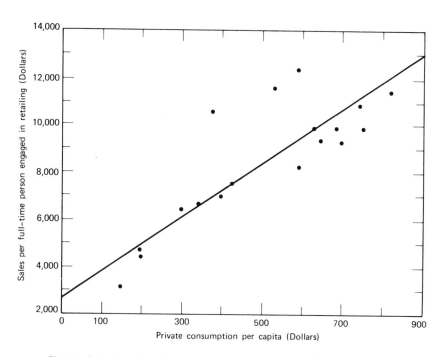

Figure 3–1 Relationship between private consumption per capita and sales per person in retailing, 1955, using official exchange rates.

account for 60 to 70% of a family's budget in low-income countries (e.g., Portugal and Greece) and 30 to 40% in more developed countries, to the purchase of clothing and durable goods.[29] Units of purchase are larger in the latter cases than in the former, thus contributing to improved marketing efficiency. Here, then, the increased personal consumption expenditure per capita (a proxy for personal income) leads to changing consumption patterns that *directly* affect efficiency.

There are other indirect linkages that account for improved efficiency. Higher incomes permit greater density of buying power in a given geographical region which, in turn, permits the development of supermarkets. Scale economies flowing from this development contribute to increased sales per person engaged in retailing. Related to this chain

[29] See James B. Jeffereys and Derek Knee, *Retailing in Europe* (London: Macmillan, 1962), p. 47 for an elaboration of this point.

of events is the linkage between per capita income growth and increased urbanization. Increased population density contributes to the massed purchasing power referred to above, and this force permits larger store size, hence improved efficiency. The Hall, Knapp, and Winsten study of distribution efficiency in Great Britain, Canada, and the United States confirms the existence of a positive correlation between town size and sales per person engaged in retailing.[30] This research suggests a final, and more subtle, connection between higher income and retail store efficiency. Higher incomes increase the mobility of customers who, seeking stores whose names are familiar, shop at chains. Since total sales per chain and sales per employee in chains exceed those of independents, efficiency in retailing is concomitantly increased.

These are a few of the subtleties that both complicate and illuminate the analysis of efficiency in trade. They should permit the reader to understand better the forces contributing to varying levels of efficiency among different countries. They also serve as a warning to avoid explanations that use first-order factors to account for efficiency differences. Appearances deceive. Causality is usually more involved than it appears to be.

A classic example of possible confusion in interpreting distribution cost data arises from a comparison of distribution costs in the United States with those in the Soviet Union. Wholesale and retail markups in the United States are about 37 to 50% of average retail prices. Goldman has estimated the comparable markups in the Soviet Union to be 19 to 29%.[31] Is the Russian distribution system, therefore, more efficient than that of the United States? Goldman finds that sales per employee in retailing in the two countries are similar—$23,790 in Russia for 1958 versus either $29,340 or $20,720 in the United States, depending on the exchange rate used.

How can we account for the apparent anomaly? Lower distribution costs in the Soviet Union result partly from the existence of fewer services and amenities—inadequate lighting, greater prevalence of queuing, limited merchandise variety, and so on. Also, Preston points up the possibility of different factor prices in the trade sectors in each country, the failure of the Soviets to account properly for the cost of

---

[30] Margaret Hall, John Knapp, and Christopher Winsten, *Distribution in Great Britain and North America* (London: Oxford University Press, 1961).

[31] Marshall I. Goldman, "The Cost and Efficiency of Distribution in the Soviet Union," in Lee E. Preston (ed.), *Social Issues in Marketing* (Glenview, Ill.: Scott, Foresman, 1968), p. 45.

capital in their nonmarket-oriented system, and the different ratios of capital to labor used in each system.[32] Looking only at costs to measure the relative efficiency of the two systems, therefore, can be misleading. This is especially true in assessing input-output relations in a service industry. Costs reflect inputs; the outputs, which reflect services rendered, may vary substantially, making an efficiency comparison ambiguous. If distribution costs in the United States exceed those in the Soviet Union but the bundle of services performed is also greater, which system delivers its "product" more efficiently? Without an accurate measure of the services performed, this question cannot be answered. And, unfortunately, we lack the information necessary to make even a reasonable estimate.

SHOPPER EFFICIENCY □ Thus far, interest has focused on efficiency in the distribution of goods and services. We have examined the performance of the distribution sector or components of it; however, opportunities exist for shifting marketing functions backward toward the producer and forward toward the consumer. This being true, we need to take a systemic view of distribution costs. This orientation requires the study of *total* distribution costs, including not only those incurred by producers and distributors but also costs imputed to consumers who may be called on to assume some marketing functions formerly performed by distributors.

Anthony Downs has spelled out the goals of consumers in the buying process.[33] Along with producers, consumers seek to maximize efficiency —the "efficiency of consumption." Consumption costs include money, time, and energy. Money costs include the cost of goods bought, transportation costs incurred in shopping, and income lost from shopping instead of engaging in remunerative work. Included in time costs are all expenditures of time in the shopping process—traveling to and from stores and time spent in selecting and paying for goods. Energy output is directly proportional to time expended in shopping, but some shoppers expend additional energy fighting traffic, arranging for baby sitters, and so on.

Consumers weigh the importance of these three factors differently depending on varying evaluations of their relative importance. Factors affecting their importance to each consumer are his income, prices of

---

[32] Preston, *Markets and Marketing: An Orientation,* p. 35.
[33] This section draws on Anthony Downs, "A Theory of Consumer Efficiency," in Lee E. Preston (ed.), *Social Issues in Marketing,* pp. 106–111.

specific goods, the degree of product standardization (standardized products economize on time spent comparing various offerings), and the time pressure under which the consumer operates. The existence of what appears to be irrational buyer behavior may stem from different weights being applied to these four factors. A wasteful expenditure of time to one shopper may represent an important price saving to another.

Downs cites a number of recent developments in retailing that have increased consumers' shopping efficiency. Among them: suburban shopping centers, which save walking time and which also create scale economies from shoppers' patronizing several stores on one shopping trip; scrambled merchandising, which makes more variety available in a single store; self-service with its attendant reduction in costs and prices; longer shopping hours, which allow several members of the family to shop together—another time economizer.

Let us examine in more detail the effect on total efficiency of some of these changes in marketing, for example, the introduction of self-service in grocery and variety stores. Here, increased efficiency at the distributor level occurs at the expense of the consumer buyer. The consumer serves himself rather than being served. Inputs under the old system consisted of labor performed by the store clerk (plus other nonlabor inputs), and shopping time expended by the customer. Much of the so-called shopping time was, in effect, waiting time. This condition continues to exist where the customer is waited on—at a gas station pump, for example. Under self-service, it is not clear whether the customer's shopping time is increased or reduced.[34] If the shopper spends no more time shopping under self-service than he did when he was provided service, then there has been no transfer in cost from the retailer to the buyer. But there is a net efficiency gain to the buyer from the existence of lower margins resulting from the retailer's reduced labor costs.

Several factors could modify this conclusion. Although the consumer may devote no more time to shopping with self-service, he performs more work and expends more energy than when service is provided. This represents a "cost" that legitimately should be balanced against the efficiency gains accruing to the retailer. Delivery is another function that is often transferred from the retailer to the customer. Again, this transfer may represent a net gain in total shopper-retailer efficiency. Avoiding delivery reduces the retailer's costs but, since the shopper

[34] Comparisons here are difficult since the product assortments in self-service and nonself-service stores are usually vastly different.

usually must return home after shopping regardless of who makes delivery, the opportunity cost of the shopper's assuming the delivery function is zero.[35] This purely economic orientation also ignores psychic "costs" to the shopper: the extra energy exerted in delivering the goods and the psychic loss from being burdened with packages.

There is another aspect to the problem. Self-service shopping thrusts a burden on the customer to increase his product knowledge. He must gain either specific product knowledge or added brand awareness. Acquiring the information involves an imputed cost measured, again, by the opportunities lost in the process. Correctly evaluating the net gain to the economy from the introduction of self-service would require an appropriate adjustment for this aggregate opportunity cost.

We face similar problems in assessing the net effect of shifting packaging functions from grocery stores, hardware stores, and other shops to the manufacturer. The shift reduces distribution costs but at the expense of manufacturers. Since packaging lends itself to scale economies, there is probably a net gain to the consumer. What he gains in lower cost, however, he loses in flexibility by having to accept a limited number of package sizes.

Self-service, as we have seen, improves marketing efficiency for distributors by shifting functional burdens to the shopper. Other marketing innovations could similarly reduce marketing costs either by curtailing services offered or by transferring some of the marketing job to shoppers. Some years ago Bressler looked for ways to increase efficiency in milk distribution. He found that cost could be cut up to 2.5¢ per quart by delivering on alternate days instead of daily.[36] Requiring consumers to buy milk in stores rather than receive alternate-day delivery could cut costs an additional 2.4¢ per quart.

Still other marketing innovations could further cut distribution costs, but at the expense of viable competitive markets. Bressler also suggested the possibility of creating exclusive dealer territories in milk distribution to reduce competitive overlap, with a possible cost savings of 2¢ per quart. And an innovation in manufacturing—the creation of dairy plant monopolies—could reduce milk costs in some towns an additional 4¢ per quart. Whether or not Bressler's cost figures are correct, it is questionable that the reduced costs would translate them-

[35] The conclusions reached here ignore the situation when shoppers phone in their orders.

[36] R. G. Bressler, Jr., *City Milk Distribution* (Cambridge, Mass.: Harvard University Press, 1952).

/

selves into lower prices. The market imperfections implicit in these two innovations would certainly lead to monopoly profits in the absence of governmental regulation.

Can we achieve a reduction in the wastes of competition without resorting to the creation of monopoly markets? Is there a compromise between "too many retailers" on the one hand and retail trade monopolies on the other? We turn now to this question and ones related to it.

TOO MANY RETAILERS? □ One of the strongest indictments of marketing is that it is wasteful. The waste is attributed to several alleged factors: excessive advertising, unnecessary product differentiation, contrived product obsolescence, and excessive resources devoted to retailing. What is the evidence to confirm or deny existence of the last factor and, if confirmed, what is the social cost of having excess retail capacity? And what social costs are associated with the high mortality rate in retailing?

Substantial excess capacity exists in most retail establishments. Customer shopping patterns pretty well dictate that it will exist. Living habits and working hours limit the shopping time available to many customers; this leads to peaks and valleys in weekly store sales. Seasonal factors cause additional sales fluctuations. Retailers have attempted to even out sales through such devices as double trading-stamp days, but most efforts produce limited success. Thus, stores are burdened with almost continuous excess capacity. The extent of the excess is evident during peak periods (e.g., the Christmas season) when sales volume far exceeds the levels achieved in slack times. Excess capacity also exists with semimechanized facilities such as vending machines which stand idle most of the time.

Measuring the extent of retail excess capacity and its social cost is almost impossible. An attempt to measure it in gasoline retailing (discussed later in the chapter) left the question pretty well unanswered. If one views a retail establishment as a conduit through which goods flow, then certainly existing facilities are capable of enormous output expansion or, conversely, far fewer physical facilities could handle a given volume. Obviously, retailers provide more than a vehicle for transferring goods from wholesale intermediaries or producers to consumers. They sell a bundle of services that accompany the transfer of goods. Limiting excess capacity within a store might reduce for some the psychic pleasure of shopping by creating congestion, queuing problems, and so on.

No matter what yardstick one uses to measure capacity in retailing, considerable excess continually exists. New firms add to capacity; others drop out through failure or for other reasons. So "wastes" exist both because of a continuing overhang of excess capacity and because of repeated failures. Defenders of the existing system argue that this waste is the price we pay to maintain viably competitive markets. Providing consumers with alternative sources of supply strengthens price competition. Maintaining ease of market entry also buttresses the free market system. It gives would-be entrepreneurs the opportunity to try— if only to fail.

Cox reminds us that we have little conclusive evidence of the inefficiencies involved in retailing's high mortality rate.[37] We assume that the social cost of repeated failures in retailing is high—that failures result in the loss of physical resources in addition to the misallocation of effort that might have been more productively expended in alternative employment. Although no data exist concerning the dollar loss from retailers' failures, we can still analyze their impact.

First we have to separate the social waste of the failure itself from the waste resulting from the aforementioned excess retail capacity. Any firm operating at less than capacity contributes to inefficiency even though it operates successfully and is in no danger of bankruptcy. However, the unsuccessful firm is likely to encounter inadequate sales or abnormally high costs (the two are usually related), both of which reflect the existence of economic waste. Thus, excessive social costs precede failure. Do they also follow from the failure itself? At first glance, they would appear to. There is visible evidence of waste when a retail establishment fails—an empty store, idle equipment, distress merchandise, and unemployed personnel. But the retail trade structure is dynamic; firms die and new ones enter continuously. Entrants often acquire the facilities of those that fail—even though the new firms may operate in different retail trades. Therefore, much of what appears to be wasted is recovered and reused. This recycling process apparently limits the extent of the economic loss—"apparently" because recycling may perpetuate inefficiency under new ownership. Failure may have stemmed from excessive overcapacity in the trade (as distinct from "normal" overcapacity) or from an unsatisfactory store location. If the successor firm operates in the same trade as the one that failed, economic waste is likely tc continue. The same is true if the location is inadequate. Eventually the physical facilities fall into disuse and society finally writes off the assets as dead losses. In the meantime, the suc-

---

[37] Cox, op. cit., p. 180.

cessor retailer uses more resources than necessary to function efficiently so that, until his demise, he burdens society with continuing economic waste.

One might argue that society is served by the process of recycling bankrupt retail trade facilities since, using a sunk costs argument, it costs nothing to use up existing facilities. Furthermore, society gains by getting the full measure of value from existent facilities. This argument ignores the wastes that might accrue from the underutilization of the uneconomic retail capacity. Given the presence of continuing excess capacity, a better alternative would call for existing firms to take up the slack.

Reducing the number of retail outlets to limit overcapacity is an appealing solution. Some years ago, Richard Lundy tackled this problem when he asked whether we had too many gas stations.[38] To answer this question requires the query: "Too many for what?" The optimum number of stations depends upon whose interest is paramount. Lundy roughly estimated the various optima, given certain assumptions. At one extreme, Lundy postulated exaggerated conditions that would minimize the number of stations. Conditions bore little resemblance to reality. He had customers buying gas 24 hours a day with no break between cars receiving service; only one brand was available; cars would arrive at the station with an empty tank and get filled up; stations would be located so as to equalize demand at each outlet. At the other extreme, conditions would solely favor the customers. For example, no customer would live more than one-half mile from a station. Other models called for enough stations to maximize station operators' profits by setting up a system of little monopolies, and for enough stations of a certain quality to maximize welfare.

Obviously the number of stations required to meet each standard varied enormously—from a minimum of 1906 stations (5718 pumps) to a maximum of at least 4.4 million stations. These totals compared with the 1.5 million pumps then (1946) in existence. Lundy's estimates are rather meaningless. The assumptions were too wild to be taken seriously and he failed to trace the second-order effects on consumption of his assumptions—for example, the impact on consumption of monopoly conditions. But the exercise is useful to point out the divergent answers to the question: "How many retailers?" It depends. It

[38] Richard D. Lundy, "How Many Service Stations Are Too Many," in Reavis Cox and Wroe Alderson, *Theory in Marketing* (Homewood, Ill.: Richard D. Irwin, 1950), pp. 321–336.

depends on how one balances the diverse needs of various elements in the economic system. Answering the question hinges on the answers to other questions. What price are we willing to pay for convenience? Can we limit entry without infringing on individuals' economic freedom? How do we balance the inefficiency stemming from excess capacity against the benefits of a vigorous competitive system?

As long as entry barriers into retailing are low, it will be hard to eliminate chronic overcapacity and to reduce substantially retailing's high mortality rate. Relieving the overcapacity problem will require reducing artificial governmental support of small retailing. Chain store taxes, fair trade and minimum markup laws, and the Robinson-Patman Act buttress the atomistic structure of retailing and contribute to its inefficiency.

Better planning, more adequate financing, and improved training may reduce the mortality rate. Many franchising operations combine these advantages to the benefit of the franchisee. Available data indicate that sound franchise establishments have higher success ratios than do traditional, independent retailers; however, there is a danger that overbuilding of franchises may lead to a continuation of the chronic overcapacity problem. The proliferation of gasoline stations, many of which are essentially franchised, demonstrates that franchising is not a panacea.

OTHER INEFFICIENCIES IN MARKETING □ So far the discussion of alleged inefficiency in marketing has centered solely on the retail sector. The charge of inefficiency goes beyond these institutions. Advertising is the obvious and inviting target of marketing's critics. Even practitioners of the profession admit to waste in advertising. Chapter 2, which analyzed the role of advertising in the economic system, discussed in detail the charge that advertising poorly serves us. To determine whether advertising involves waste requires an assessment of its *net* effect on the system. Its defenders point to the role that advertising performs in maintaining a competitive economy, in lowering production costs, and promoting new products. One must balance these advantages against the apparent waste of resources to get a better perspective on advertising's alleged inefficiencies.

Personal selling (outside of that done by retailers) is another area that needs scrutiny. There are various ways to reduce selling expenses. One is to change the organizational structure in distribution. The typical consumer is aware of personal selling that involves his coming into direct contact with a salesman. He may be unaware of selling down the channel—for example, wholesalers selling to retailers, or industrial salesmen selling to jobbers in other wholesale intermediaries. Establishing corporate chains and retailer co-ops can eliminate some of this selling effort. So too can other efforts to rationalize distribution through vertical integration. Increasing seller concentration at the manufacturing level may also reduce the total selling effort. These moves, however, may exact a toll in the form of higher prices growing out of increased market power. Much could undoubtedly be accomplished to reduce firms' personal selling costs through improved salesmen's routing, better call-account management, and alternative ways of handling small orders. Some firms have cut selling costs substantially by using operations research techniques and distribution cost analysis, but much remains to be done.[39] The failure of many firms to control selling costs as effectively as they control factory costs undoubtedly leads to higher than necessary selling costs.

Summarizing, firms may reduce personal selling costs in two ways: by improving efficiency at the firm level through better management and by rationalization of the institutional structure through vertical integration within the channel or by horizontal integration of producers or distributors. Again, the second of these alternatives creates the same dilemma as before: How do we accomplish marketing economies without unduly weakening competition?

SUMMARY AND CONCLUSIONS □ Answering the question whether marketing costs too much is not an easy task. First there are important definitional problems. Are we concerned with technical efficiency, economic efficiency, or what Preston calls "innovative" efficiency—"the effectiveness of the marketing unit, firm, or system in making . . . choices among both existing and potential alternatives."[40] One must decide what inputs to measure and how to measure them. Outputs create more of a problem. Marketing is involved with the delivery of a bundle of functions or services. These shift over time—some shift from distributor to producer, others shift forward to the consumer. So the output varies not only from changes in the volume of goods moving through the marketing system but also from the changing services performed by marketers in the discharge of their duties.

---

[39] See, for example, Charles H. Sevin, *How Manufacturers Reduce Their Distribution Costs* (U.S. Department of Commerce, 1948); and Arthur A. Brown, Frank T. Hulswit, and John D. Kettelle, "A Study of Sales Operations," *Operations Research* (June 1956), pp. 296–308.

[40] Preston, *Markets and Marketing: An Orientation,* p. 32.

Fairly assessing marketing efficiency suffers from another problem. What improves efficiency for a firm may not add to macro marketing efficiency. Take the case of a firm that increases its advertising budget. If effective, the increase might add to the firm's profits by lowering both per unit production and marketing costs. The higher advertising budget might have a dual impact on marketing costs. It might reduce the per unit advertising costs by increasing its effectiveness, but it might also reduce unit selling costs by reinforcing the selling effort and making it more effective. But what impact does this increased marketing efficiency have on rival firms? With rising demand, increased sales of one firm need not detract from another's; however, in stagnant or declining markets, losses in competitors' marketing effectiveness may offset the gains from the increased advertising.

The long-term productivity data in distribution show a fairly constant trend in the share of the consumer's dollar devoted to distribution (in recent decades), and a steady, but slow, growth in labor productivity. The lag in productivity in distribution versus productivity growth in other sectors has led to a steadily rising share of the total labor force engaged in distribution. This appears to be an international phenomenon.

This observation leads to an apparent contradiction. How do we reconcile the relatively fixed percentage of the total sales dollar going to distribution with a growing share of labor resources devoted to trade? The answer lies in an affirmation of the theory of marginal productivity. This cornerstone of economic theory holds that factors of production are paid on the basis of their marginal contribution to output. Thus, we would expect a factor such as labor engaged in retail trade, where productivity lags behind productivity in other sectors, to receive correspondingly low wages. This is generally the case. Therefore, although more labor moves into the trade sector as it grows, the lower level of compensation there keeps the share of economic activity in trade relatively constant, when expressed in *dollar* terms.

Whether the United States economy or other essentially free enterprise systems devote excessive resources to marketing remains an unsettled question. Certainly there is room for reduction both in the numbers of distribution entities (retailers, wholesalers, and so on) as well as in the quantity of advertising, selling, and other marketing functions. Even marketing's strongest supporters admit to waste in the present arrangement. What remains unclear is how sharply we can contract marketing's functions without tampering with the essence of a free market system. Waste, therefore, may be a by-product of a free enterprise economy. How much of it can we afford? How much of it will an increasingly socially conscious society permit? These appear to be the crucial, unanswered questions.

□ DISCUSSION QUESTIONS □

1. Compare and contrast the problems associated with measuring productivity in the distribution and the manufacturing sectors.

2. What is the "micro-macro" conflict? Give several examples of the conflict?

3. How many gas stations should there "ideally" be in the area where you live? Draw up a model stating your assumptions concerning such things as grades handled, number of pumps, waiting time, etc.

4. Which aspects of marketing are amenable to productivity measurements and which are not?

5. Would a reduction in unit marketing costs necessarily reduce total unit costs? Defend your answer.

6. Make two lists of recent (last several decades) innovations in marketing: one of those that probably resulted in lower marketing costs, the other of those that probably increased marketing costs.

7. Think of at least one area of marketing (other than gasoline retailing) that might profit by improved productivity. Suggest one or more ways to increase productivity in that sector and be prepared to defend your proposal. Does your proposal sacrifice customer convenience and satisfaction to achieve greater efficiency?

8. Why do hourly, daily, and seasonal peaks and valleys occur in retailing? Can you think of feasible ways to even out the fluctuations? Would your suggestions improve customer welfare?

9. Think of a retailer in your locality whom you would characterize as inefficient. Think of another whom you would label "efficient." What makes the one efficient and the other inefficient? Do you patronize both retailers? If you shop at the inefficient store, why do you do so?

10. Think of a retail establishment in your locality that has changed hands in recent years, apparently from financial failure. How much economic waste has attended the failure, and what form did it take?

11. Wages in retailing traditionally have been lower than in many other occupations. How would you account for this phenomenon?

12. Do efforts to improve retailing efficiency make it harder for small retailers to survive? Explain.

4

Consumerism

One of the abiding questions confronting a democratic society is the extent to which it tolerates or encourages government intervention in the marketplace. The response to this issue may well change over time. In the United States—following the English tradition—the trend has moved toward increased government intervention. The laissez-faire attitude in the 19th century has made way for the welfare state of the mid-20th century. The shift has been uneven. Moves toward government intervention have come in spurts, with occasional bursts of legislative activity followed by a period of quiescence. Much of this legislation has been directed toward protecting the consumer from the perils of the marketplace.

The last few years have witnessed a resurgence in consumer-protective legislation and administrative action which we label "The Consumerism Movement." This chapter and the following one study this movement. They trace its origins and compare it with previous activity of this type and, in the process, analyze various legislative and administrative actions and proposals designed to protect consumer interests. The field is too broad to permit an encyclopedic account of deficiencies in the marketing system and the government's reactions to them. These chapters deal with some of the important issues that have captured public attention. But the treatment transcends those issues that have generated actual or threatened government intervention, to include several issues that concern consumers but that have not yet resulted in government intervention. Among them are product differentiation and branding, planned product obsolescence, and several pricing issues. Before studying these and other areas of consumer interest, let us put the current consumer movement in perspective by looking at its antecedents and at the shift in the public's attitude toward intervention in the marketplace.

HISTORY OF GOVERNMENT INTERVENTION □ For centuries the rule of the market was *caveat emptor* (let the buyer beware). This concept, which we tend to associate with 19th-century economic liberalism, actually dates back to the Middle Ages. Trade then was sparse and usually occurred in local markets and at fairs. The buyer could inspect goods he intended to buy. His judgment and visual inspections served him better than the integrity of the seller who might move on and never be seen again. Caveat emptor summed up the ground rules that governed these occasional transactions. A buyer might secure legal relief from fraudulent transactions only if the seller gave express warranties that were violated; yet, even in these cases, the seller was not liable if the buyer's inspection could reveal the falsity of the warranties. Thus the buyer of an obviously lame horse had no legal redress against a seller who warranted the horse's physical soundness if inspection would have revealed the animal's deficiency.

By the early part of the 19th century conditions had modified the concept of caveat emptor. By then trade had greatly increased, especially in England whose economy burgeoned following the onset of the Industrial Revolution. Increasingly, goods were sold on the basis of samples or by description, without benefit of inspection. As opportunities for fraud increased, so did the need to protect innocent buyers. Although caveat emptor continued to survive, increasing court victories for plaintiffs in misrepresentation cases weakened it. The courts moved farther away from caveat emptor by invoking the doctrine of implied warranty, which imputed a warranty to goods purchased even when sellers avoided an expressed warranty. In England, the Sales of Goods Act in 1893 codified protection of the consumer and pretty effectively killed caveat emptor. Court decisions in the United States accomplished the same end.

Although we can trace caveat emptor back to the Middle Ages, we associate it with more recent commercial history when trading activity increased. Indeed, caveat emptor and the doctrine of laissez-faire, which dominated economic thought through much of the 19th century, are quite compatible. As long as laissez-faire dominated economic thinking, there was little room for consumer-protective legislation. The breakthrough on this front in the United States came in 1872 with passage of the Mail Fraud Act. This act, designed to protect consumers from fraudulent schemes peddled through the mails, was the only piece of consumer legislation passed in the United States in the 19th century.[1]

[1] James Bishop, Jr. and Henry W. Hubbard, *Let the Seller Beware* (Washington: The National Press, 1969), p. 25.

Aside from the Mail Fraud Act, other early departures from laissez-faire were designed more to protect industry from itself than to protect the consumer. The Interstate Commerce Commission Act of 1887 grew out of attempts at collusion among railroads and discrimination in rate making, but its passage also followed a period of ruinous competition among carriers which weakened them economically. Similarly the Sherman Act of 1890, designed to control monopolies, stemmed from a history of predatory tactics and collusion practiced by powerful trusts that dominated several industries toward the end of the 19th century.

The Federal Trade Commission Act and the Clayton Act, both passed in 1914, also sought to regulate competition. Although they indirectly benefited consumers, their immediate impact was felt by business firms. The only other laws during this era to benefit the consumer directly were the Pure Food and Drug Act (1906) and the Meat Inspection Act (1907). These laws ended legislative activity in the consumer area until the 1930s. In the intervening period, America's preoccupation with World War I and the prosperity of the 1920s insulated its citizens from reform proposals.

The depression of the 1930s spawned the Securities and Exchange Commission Act in 1934 which, among other things, increased information available to purchasers of securities, and the 1938 Federal Food, Drug and Cosmetic Act, which sought to prevent adulteration and misbranding of products covered by the law. Other legislation forbidding misrepresentation and requiring disclosure of information useful to the consumer included labeling and price disclosure acts covering wool products (1939), fur products (1951), textile fibers (1958), and automobiles (1958).

The 1960s ushered in another era of renewed interest in consumer protection. Attention centered principally on safety and disclosure of information. In regard to safety, legislation included the Child Protection Law (1966) to regulate the sale and use of hazardous substances and toys, the Natural Gas Pipeline Safety Act (1968), the National Traffic and Motor Vehicle Safety Act (1966), which permits establishing federal safety standards for automobiles, a tighter meat inspection law (1967), and an amendment to the Flammable Fabrics Act (1967), extending coverage of the original 1953 law to include nonclothing fabrics. To better inform the consumer, Congress passed the Kefauver-Harris Drug bill (1962), which required labeling drugs by generic name, the Truth-in-Packaging (1966) and Truth-in-Lending (1968) Acts, and the Public Health Cigarette Smoking Act (1970). The latter act, motivated by safety and informational factors, banned cigarette commercials on television and radio and required a stiffer warning statement on cigarette packages concerning the dangers of smoking. In addition, administrative action has advanced the consumerism movement in a number of areas. Examples are the Commerce Department's authority to set safety and grading standards for tires and the F.T.C.'s tire advertising guides which furnish consumers with useful tire performance information. We shall discuss some of these laws and administrative actions in more detail in the next chapter.

What explains the spread of today's consumer movement? Aaker and Day cite five reasons.

1. Increased consumer confusion stemming from the greater variety of available goods and brands, and exposure to deceptive or uninformative advertising.

2. A higher level of consumer expectations concerning product quality.

3. Suspicion generated by disclosures of questionable business practices in certain industries (e.g., pharmaceuticals).

4. Increased concern for the poor who are often most acutely affected by shoddy business practices.

5. Heightened concern for the quality of life which brings the entire market system under scrutiny and criticism.[2]

Others attribute the consumerism movement to additional factors. The increased complexity of new products (in addition to their greater number) is thought to make buying decisions more difficult. The impersonality of dealing with today's giant corporations is also said to contribute to the consumer's displeasure.[3] It is ironic that consumerism has flourished during a period when American manufacturers increasingly have adopted the "marketing concept," which shapes products and marketing strategies to satisfy consumer needs.

Observers of marketing behavior with long memories may have a feeling of déjà vu as they study the current consumerism movement. Several of the factors accounting for today's version of consumerism contributed to growth of the consumer movement during the 1930s.

[2] David A. Aaker and George S. Day (eds.), *Consumerism: Search for the Consumer Interest,* pp. 9–10.

[3] "Consumerism: A New and Growing Force in the Marketplace," (3rd ed.), Burson-Marsteller, March 1970, p. 20.

Looking back to that period, Duddy and Revzan noted the increased number and variety of products, "the pressures of advertising, much of it misleading, some of it untruthful, all of it aggressive."[4] The depression of the 1930s also made the consumer more aware of prices. Undoubtedly, the "Nixon recession" and the accompanying accelerated inflation have had a similar impact recently.

All the bursts of consumerism in the United States have had one thing in common: extensive publicity concerning the alleged business and market evils, which has stimulated government action. Publicity has been generated either by events that outraged the public or books demonstrating the need for reform. Upton Sinclair's novel, *The Jungle,* which dramatized the unsavory aspects of meat packing at the beginning of the 20th century, led to passage of the Meat Inspection Act. His accounts of filth in the meat packing plants and the sale of diseased cattle as clean meat were designed to elicit support for Sinclair's socialist causes. His efforts bore fruit but they missed his target. Sinclair later lamented, "I aimed for the nation's heart and hit its stomach instead."[5] During the same period the persistent efforts of Dr. Harvey W. Wiley to publicize the adulteration of food products paid off with passage of the Pure Food and Drug Act.

The next wave of interest in consumerism owed much to the publication of two books, *Your Money's Worth* (1927) by Stuart Chase and F. J. Schlink and *100,000,000 Guinea Pigs* (1931) by Schlink and Arthur Kallet. Consumer's Research, Inc., and the Consumers' Union, both designed to help consumers with their buying decisions, grew out of these publications. A few years later the Food, Drug and Cosmetic Act, which required drug companies to prove the safety of their products before the F.D.A. would authorize their use, stemmed directly from the shock generated by the deaths of over 100 people who consumed a lethal patent medicine. Senator Kefauver's drug bill in 1962 similarly got a boost from a drug "horror story"—the deformation of babies born to women who had used the tranquilizer thalidomide while pregnant.

CURRENT CONSUMER MOVEMENT □ In the 1960s, Ralph Nader, bursting on the scene with his condemnation of auto manufacturers, *Unsafe at Any Speed,* paved the way for the auto safety bill. His book

[4] Edward A. Duddy and David A. Revzan, *Marketing* (New York: McGraw-Hill Book Co., Inc., 1947), p. 138.
[5] Reported in Bishop and Hubbard, op. cit., p. 35.

was the opening salvo in a continuing battle for consumer protection begun by Nader and carried on by his "Raiders."

The current consumer movement dates back to the beginning of the Kennedy administration. Now over a decade old, it shows no sign of diminishing in intensity. What accounts for its success and relative longevity? Several features of today's consumerism distinguish it from previous movements.[6] First, there are the quality and characteristics of current consumer advocates. They are pragmatists, not idealists. They seek to work through the system and change it rather than destroy it. Ralph Nader, for example, lacks Upton Sinclair's devotion to socialism and, while he is a vocal and articulate critic of present business practices, he appeals more to reason than to the emotion found in some earlier consumerism literature. Second, consumerism is a popular political issue. Even if the issue fails to help a politician, advocacy of consumerism doesn't seem to hurt him either. This condition permits politicians with strongly held pro-consumer sentiments to advocate pet causes without fear of political harm. Finally, the present consumer movement is being institutionalized both at federal and state levels. Out of President Kennedy's Consumer Advisory Council has evolved the Office of the Special Assistant to the President for Consumer Affairs, which deals exclusively with consumer matters. Various states have also established consumer bureaus and committees to represent consumer interests.

Most previous attempts to create government bodies to represent consumer interests have been expedients introduced during war or depression. The act creating the N.R.A. in 1933 provided for a Consumers' Advisory Board to protect consumers' interests which prosecution of the act might violate. Both the O.P.A. and O.P.S. during World War II and the Korean War also had consumer divisions. For several years the Council of Economic Advisors consulted with a Consumer Advisory Committee. All of these bodies were short-lived and relatively ineffective. They suffered from inadequate staffing and financing and from the possession of limited authority.

Some trace the beginning of the present consumer movement to President Kennedy's Special Message in March 1962, on Protecting the Consumer Interest, when he enunciated the consumer's four "rights." These rights, to be assured by the government, were:[7]

---

6 See Bishop and Hubbard, ibid., for a discussion of these points.
7 "Consumer Advisory Council First Report," October 1963, pp. 6–28.

1. *"The right to safety*—to be protected against the marketing of goods which are hazardous to health or life." This is a partial recognition of the move from *caveat emptor* to a philosophy that holds sellers accountable for the consequences of their actions. It articulates the rationale for legislation concerning food, drugs, cosmetics, and other goods, which is designed to protect consumer health and welfare.

2. *"The right to be informed*—to be protected against fraudulent, deceitful or grossly misleading information, advertising, labeling or other practices, and to be given the facts he needs to make an informed choice." Over the years this right has been secured for the consumer under the free disclosure provisions of the Securities and Exchange Commission Act, the specification of standard weights and measures, grade labeling requirements, labeling acts, provisions for the identity, product composition, and quality of insecticides, drugs, poisons, alcoholic beverages, and so on.

3. *"The right to choose*—to be assured, whenever possible, of access to a variety of products and services at competitive prices, and in those industries in which competition is not workable and government regulation is substituted, to be assured satisfactory quality and service at fair prices." Most of the legislation providing this protection dates back a number of years, beginning with the I.C.C. Act and including the Sherman Act, Clayton Act, Federal Trade Commission Act, Robinson-Patman Act, the Wheeler-Lea Act, and the Cellar amendment to the Clayton Act.

4. *"The right to be heard*—to be assured that consumer interests will receive full and sympathetic consideration in the formulation of governmental policy, and fair and expeditious treatment in its administrative tribunals." The existence of millions of consumers and billions of annual transactions makes the guarantee of this right difficult to achieve. Consumers generally lack the organization to make their collective voices heard in the executive and legislative branches of government. The office of the Special Assistant to the President for Consumer Affairs, previously referred to, represents a forum that gives the consumer a voice in consumer matters. More effective probably are groups such as "Nader's Raiders" which, through a few activists, seek

remedies for the mass of consumers. Their success with several issues points up the potential influence that a small, organized, informed consumer group can have on government policies.

In broad outline, President Kennedy's statement sets forth the dimensions of the consumer movement. Ralph Nader, who is on the front line of the battle, has considered the *specific* shape that consumerism ought to take. The following is a list of what he thinks should be done to improve the consumer's position.[8]

1. Good, fast disclosure of product information concerning quality, quantity, and safety. The consumer needs the information to help evaluate competitive products.
2. The strengthening of efforts to recall defective products and to refund payments for unsatisfactory purchases.
3. Fairer court rules and better legal representation for the economically deprived.
4. More government safety standards and a continual updating of them as products and technology change. Needed also is improved enforcement of existing laws.
5. Government (or government-sponsored) research to improve product safety.
6. Better protection from price-fixing and "product-fixing"—the calculated restraint of innovation to protect present product positions.
7. More work by technical and professional societies to improve products and aid in the solution of environmental problems.
8. More private interest groups and government agencies designed to protect the consumer.

Another way to promote consumer interests, which the foregoing list ignores, is by self-regulation through industry associations. Often an industry group can initiate policies or impose standards that individual firms are reluctant to adopt unilaterally for fear of being handicapped competitively. Some of this industry activity already exists. The motion picture industry's self-regulation dates back to the 1920s. For years the industry censored itself through the so-called Hays Office. Recently

---

[8] Ralph Nader, "The Great American Gyp," in Aaker and Day, op. cit., pp. 48–57.

the industry has sought to rate movies to indicate their desirability for different age groups. Criticized on several counts, the rating system nonetheless attempts to meet some of the consumer's informational needs concerning the industry's "product."

On a broader scale, a Council of Better Business Bureaus has grown out of several national Better Business Bureau organizations with the goal of strengthening and standardizing local bureau activities, and especially improving the servicing of local consumer complaints. The local bureaus have long suffered from inadequate funding and have been accused of protecting local businesses more than the consumer. The council's extensive fund-raising drive in 1971 sought to relieve the bureau's shortcomings and to make them a more responsive force for consumer protection.[9]

The Grocery Manufacturers of America responded to the pressures of the consumer movement in another way. It appointed a Council on Consumer Affairs, which identified potential industry problem areas as they related to consumer concerns. Analyzing charges leveled against the food industry, the council realized that it could not determine which were and which were not legitimate. Thus it established in 1967 a Consumer Research Institute "to sponsor and/or conduct research in any area of marketing practice that may be the subject of consumer concern for the purpose of shaping public policy."[10]

These three examples illustrate the kinds of industry response to the consumer protection movement. One could cite other cases of industry cooperation in this area. In toto, however, these efforts fall far short of providing adequate consumer protection, although the potential of the industry-wide approach obviously has not been fully tapped.

President Kennedy's general guidelines and Ralph Nader's specific suggestions for protection of the consumer, previously referred to, raise an important philosophical question. What should be the government's role in defending the consumer in the marketplace and redressing whatever imbalances exist in market transactions? Long ago we moved away from the laissez-faire, caveat emptor doctrine at one end of the spectrum. It is not clear what lies at the other end. A socialist state governed by central decision making will not necessarily make the consumer's interests paramount.

Laissez-faire advocates argue that the force of competition protects

[9] "Better Business Unit Starts National Drive to Upgrade Services," *Wall Street Journal*, December 3, 1970, p. 7.

[10] Donald M. Kendall, "Industry and Consumer," *Dun's Review* (September 1969), pp. 111–112.

the consumer's welfare. If a seller offers shoddy or unsafe merchandise, exaggerates claims, or provides deceptive or extortionate credit terms, the consumer soon discovers it and transfers his patronage elsewhere. In many market situations, however, this buyer option has been an ineffective penalty. This is especially true in the sale of high-priced goods that are seldom purchased. Furthermore, many consumers, through ignorance or otherwise, may be incapable of detecting fraud or misrepresentation. This condition occurs in the ghetto where uninformed or illiterate consumers buy goods whose terms of sale are unclear to them and whose purchase may put them into a tighter financial straightjacket. Finally, even the existence of vigorous competition does not insure equitable treatment for the consumer. For example, intense price competition exists in the retail sale of tires, yet the profusion of sizes and grades of tires thoroughly confuses the average buyer. The nature of the product makes its comparative evaluation difficult for most consumers. Casual inspection of a tire reveals little difference between a low-grade and premium product. And the product lasts long enough to make checking performance difficult.

The voices demanding completely unfettered competition grow weaker as time passes. Public policy in the United States has called for increasing government intervention on behalf of the consumer. Through our legislation we seem to be saying that the government's protection of the consumer from business should take several forms: the provision of safety from potentially harmful products and of information to improve buying decisions, protection against fraud and deceit, and the maintenance of competition in the marketplace. Some legislation has passed in the last nine decades to deal with these matters. Every year additional proposals are suggested to cope with one or more of these areas. In addition, there is an apparent trend toward proposals geared to protect the consumer against himself—to require motorcyclists to wear helmets when driving, to provide for fastening the driver's seat belt before one can operate a car, to allow buyers of goods sold door-to-door a grace period for rescinding the sale with no penalty.

Each reader probably has his own idea of the extent to which government ought to intervene in market affairs. Every government action in this area involves the diminution of someone's freedom to act in the (presumed) greater interests of others. Government intervention to protect the consumer usually restricts the sellers' freedom. The provision of safety standards for products or requirements for testing drugs before F.D.A. approval are cases in point. Some proposals for protecting the individual against himself—for example, mandatory wearing of helmets by motorcyclists—may restrict the individual's freedom of choice without affecting the seller at all.[11] Many consumers may find themselves applauding moves that protect their interests in the market—where they recognize the need for protection—and denouncing those that "go too far." How far, one might ask, should the government go to protect people from their own mistakes? How does one weigh the net effect upon the freedom of action of the majority of a protective measure needed for the welfare of a minority? These are the kinds of questions that consumer-oriented legislation invokes.

□ DISCUSSION QUESTIONS □

1. What role should the government play in the protection of consumer interests?

2. If you worked as a salesman for a company whose advertising misrepresented the products you sold, would you try to correct the misconceptions either by notifying your customers or by complaining about the policy to your boss? If not, why not?

3. Is a firm's concern for social responsibility consistent with a profit-maximizing policy? Explain.

4. What is the role of the business firm in society? Should it differ from what it now is? If so, in what way? Will society be better or worse off, on balance, given a changed role for business? What criteria of "goodness" do you use in formulating your answer?

5. Cite a company recently in the news that, in your opinion, is effectively fulfilling its social responsibility, and one that is not.

6. Set up a checklist for the two companies cited in the previous problem showing whether the following parties' welfare is improved, worsened, or unaffected by the firms' posture on social responsibility:

[11] This argument ignores the possible adverse effect on motorcycle sales of requiring the supplemental purchase of helmets, which effectively raises the cost of motorcycle ownership and, possibly, reduces sales.

    a. Each company's employees.
    b. Each company's stockholders.
    c. Each company's customers.
    d. The public-at-large.

7. If you were a large firm's public relations manager, what policy would you recommend to the president of the company concerning the firm's reaction to the consumerism movement?

8. On balance, has Ralph Nader been a boon or a bane to the American society? To American business?

9. Two manufacturers of desk-top mini-computers require output paper tapes with slightly different widths. Users suspect that the differences may have been deliberately designed into the products to insure the customers' purchase of each company's tapes. If their suppositions are correct, do you condemn the practice or praise the companies' management for astute marketing? If you condemn such practices, are there feasible ways to curtail them? Should the government regulate such practices? If so, how might they accomplish the regulation?

10. In a letter to the *Wall Street Journal* (November 17, 1971), Mr. Fred P. Murphy, Chairman of the Executive Committee of Grolier Inc., wrote:

"The fundamental question to be answered is this: Is it the proper role of government to take the consumer by the hand and lead him through every commercial transaction in which he may find himself involved? I submit that this type of governmental approach, which is really the basis for most of today's consumer activism, produces an unenlightened and dependent consumer, which is directly opposed to what I feel is the proper goal of creating an informed and independent consuming public."

Do you agree with this statement?

5

Consumer Issues

Some of the questions raised at the close of the last chapter get to the heart of many consumer issues. This chapter discusses those issues that have resulted in recently enacted laws and those that have generated consumer concern and thus are subject to possible future legislation. Because of the delay between writing a book and its publication, the chapter may refer to proposals that have already become legislation or, alternatively, those that have moved into limbo. However, we are more interested in understanding the dimensions of consumer concerns and suggestions for dealing with them, than in cataloguing legislative proposals. The discussion divides into four parts—an analysis of measures dealing with product, information and promotion, selling, and pricing.

PRODUCT □ This section is concerned with six topics: safety, warranties, ecological considerations, product differentiation and branding, planned obsolescence, and packaging.

PRODUCT SAFETY The precedent for legislating product safety goes at least as far back as passage of the Pure Food and Drug Act in 1906. Since then, advances in this area have paralleled and built upon what came before. Most of the recent legislative activity concerning product safety amends previous safety legislation, but in a couple of cases, it opens up new territory.

Recent years have seen the following legislation.

• Several amendments to the Federal Hazardous Substances Act to ban the sale of toys and other products intended for use by children, if they present an electrical, mechanical, or thermal hazard (1966 and 1969).

• An amendment to the Flammable Fabrics Act (1967) to expand consumer protection against such injurious flammable fabrics as draperies, curtains, and rugs.

•   The Poison Prevention Packaging Act of 1970 which provides that the Secretary of Health, Education and Welfare "may establish . . . by regulation, standards for the special packaging of any household substance if he finds that . . . the degree or nature of the hazard to children in the availability of such substance, by reason of its packaging, is such that special packaging is required to protect children from serious personal injury or serious illness resulting from handling, using or ingesting such substance."[1]

•   A law requiring the Secretary of Transportation to establish minimum federal safety standards for the transportation of gas and for pipeline facilities (1968). This legislation grew out of Nader's exposure of the safety hazard of gas pipelines.

•   Also following Nader's publicity, a law that lets the Secretary of Commerce set motor vehicle safety standards and forbids the sale of cars that fail to meet the standards. The law also authorizes research and testing to help carry out the law's mandate. Additionally, it provides for information useful to tire buyers. It calls for labeling tires, providing the buyer with information on the number of plies in a tire, composition of ply material, maximum permissible load for the tire, and identification of the manufacturer. Other legislation governing automobile safety is bound to build upon what already exists just as Congress has added to the original legislative coverage of food, drugs, cosmetics, flammable fabrics, and other hazardous substances. For example, in 1971 Senator Hart proposed a bill that would require all new cars to be equipped with bumpers that can withstand a 5 mph crash, and would provide for a system of diagnostic centers to determine the condition of cars before their purchase.

PRODUCT WARRANTIES Far from reassuring consumers of product reliability, product warranties are often sources of concern to consumers and of conflict between them, retailers, and manufacturers. Retailers usually feel the brunt of consumer complaints about inadequate products and unsatisfactory warranty treatment. Some manufacturers feel that responsibility for warranty service should rest with the retailer as an incentive to provide satisfactory installation or repair of products (especially appliances).[2] Retailers, in turn, feel that the war-

---

1 Public Law 91-601, 91st Congress, S. 2162, December 30, 1970, p. 1.
2 See testimony in U.S. Senate, Consumer Subcommittee on Commerce, *Hearings on Consumer Products Guaranty Act,* 91st Congress, 2nd Session.

ranty burden should rest with the manufacturer whose promotion may have induced the consumer to buy the product in the first place.

Pointing up the consumer's problem with warranties, a representative of Consumer's Union argues that there is a "problem of misrepresentation as to what the guarantee is all about. 'Lifetime guarantee,' 'unconditional guarantee,' 'fully guaranteed' and just plain 'guaranteed' are words skillfully used by manufacturers and retailers as part of the sales pitch. If at the point of sale, the consumer makes genuine effort to cut through the verbiage to see what it is that is being guaranteed, more often than not he is confronted with a legal document which he does not—and cannot be expected to—fully comprehend. Moreover, any written guarantee is extended to him on a take-it-or-leave-it basis. There is . . . no negotiation over the terms of the guarantee."[3] This is a consumer advocate's indictment of warranties. What are the consumers', manufacturers', and retailers' points of view?

Consumer.   He complains about:

- Faulty products with parts that break and fail prematurely.
- Unreasonable delays in retailers or manufacturers making repairs.
- The "problem" dealer who is supposed to make repairs under warranties but cannot because he has moved, is out of business, or no longer carries the warranted brand.
- Exorbitant labor charges where the warranty covers parts but requires the buyer to absorb labor charges.
- Manufacturers failing to respond satisfactorily to complaints about product quality.

Manufacturer.   He claims that:

- He tends to recall defective goods.
- He is handicapped by a shortage of qualified technicians to repair products.
- Consumers are often the source of the problem through their failure to read instructions.
- Part of the problem is the dealer who carries insufficient repair parts because he handles more than one manufacturer's line of products.

[3] Ibid., p. 256.

• Competition has forced manufacturers to produce more elaborate products with fancier features, and this product complexity has enlarged the problem.

Retailer. He argues that:

• It is difficult to hire and keep good repairmen.

• There is inadequate quality control at the manufacturer's level.

• Fussy customers—many of whom have not read operating instructions—require him to make unnecessary service calls.

• Customers exacerbate the problem by abusing the warranted products.

• Too much of the financial burden of the warranty rests with the retailer.[4]

Several bills have been introduced to correct some of these alleged inequities. One would require manufacturers to correct defective products covered by guarantees within a reasonable period of time, free of charge. The Consumer Product Warranties and F.T.C. Improvement Act of 1971 is broader. Among other things it would call for full disclosure of the warranty to be written in simple language and to spell out who is the warrantor, what products or parts are covered by the warranty, what the warrantor is obliged to do in the event of a product defect (and who pays to have it repaired), how long the warranty applies, and what are the obligations of the buyer, if any. The bill would also provide for consumer remedies for violation of warranty or service contract obligations.

The implications of such bills are enormous. They open up vastly more business transactions to governmental scrutiny than was true heretofore. The same situation exists with respect to one or two other recent pieces of consumer legislation. In previous years most legislation regulating business conduct either affected transactions between firms or, if between firm and customer, it covered actions affecting consumers as a class and not as individuals. An example of the first class of legislation is the Robinson-Patman Act which prevents price discrimination in transactions between businesses; the Pure Food and

---

4 Federal Trade Commission, *Report of the Task Force on Appliance Warranties and Service,* January 1968, reprinted in David A. Aaker and George S. Day (eds.), *Consumerism: Search for the Consumer Interest,* pp. 259–275.

Drug Act, protecting all consumers from adulterated food products, characterizes the second type of legislation. Even in these cases, enforcement of legislation is profoundly complex. Consider the millions of transactions that are subject to these laws' provisions. No one pretends that enforcement is complete. The staffs available for enforcement are hopelessly inadequate to monitor the transactions and relationships that might result in violations of the laws. Now imagine the complexity of policing laws that give *individual consumers* redress for alleged mishandling of warranties whose number runs into the tens or hundreds of millions each year!

The pressure for government activity to improve warranty protection will probably continue unless voluntary action by manufacturers and distributors blunts the need for corrective measures. The Whirlpool Corporation has introduced innovations that alleviate two of the consumers' problems with warranties.[5] First it has replaced the typically forbidding warranty, couched in legalese, with a standard letter to the customer that spells out the warranty's terms simply and succinctly. It has buttressed the improved warranty with the installation of a "cool line," which permits giving the customer information about her nearest Whirlpool service source or, alternatively, provides her with technical information that she may require. In the event of a serious service breakdown, the company, in rare instances, may respond by dispatching a field service representative to help the customer.

Whirlpool's simplification of the warranty triggered a trend among white goods manufacturers. A majority of major appliance manufacturers have adopted simpler and more comprehensive warranties.[6] The new warranties tend to have several features in common: they are shorter than the older versions, more simply written—freer of legalese, and more prominently featured. Rather than being buried in fine print on the back page of the owner's manual, the warranty now appears up front, and one's attention is drawn to it.

ECOLOGICAL CONSIDERATIONS There are few issues in the early 1970's that have captured more attention in the United States than problems related to ecology. Rachel Carson and a few other prophetic voices sounded the warning but few listened. However, a

[5] Stephen E. Upton, "The Use of Product Warranties and Guarantees as a Marketing Tool," address to the American Marketing Association, Cleveland, Ohio, December 11, 1969, reprinted in Aaker and Day (eds.), op. cit., pp. 277–282.

[6] Opinion of Mr. Sheldon Lee, Marketing Research Department, Whirlpool Corporation, who has studied the hard goods industry's warranties.

combination of factors—the perceptible worsening of the environmental problems and a heightened concern for the quality of life—has moved ecological considerations up to the front burner. Industry now finds its actions increasingly scrutinized and judged in terms of its performance in this area.

Attention centers on air and water pollution. The fouling of the environment is a by-product both of the consumption of certain products and of various production processes. Consumption of gasoline in automobile engines pollutes the atmosphere. The disposal of detergents contributes to the eutrophication of lakes and slow-moving streams. Litter from disposable containers fouls the countryside. The environmentally harmful side effects of various production processes are legion: air pollution from stack gases and particulates being spewed from industrial smokestacks; water pollution from the indiscriminate outpouring of waste products from chemical and steel manufacturing production processes; the despoiling of the countryside and polluting of adjacent bodies of water from strip coal mining. The intense concern for ecological problems by interested citizens, action groups, and various governmental agencies creates an obligation on industry to deal effectively with them. Not only will products have to meet the test of the marketplace but they will also have to satisfy ecological concerns if they are to pass muster.

Early experience with attempts to improve the environment shows that corrective action will not be easy. The detergent case illustrates the complexity of the problem. Phosphorus in detergents helps cause the eutrophication of bodies of water. This has led some federal government agencies and administrators to discourage the use of phosphates in cleaning compounds and some local and state governments to propose banning their use. Detergent manufacturers have reacted to these moves by lobbying against the restraints on the one hand and introducing substitute products on the other. But evidence points to possible deleterious effects from the caustic properties of the substitute products. Some government officials cite the danger to children of inhaling or eating the caustic compounds. Others feel that proper labeling and packaging could minimize this threat. Also, some in government urge a "go slow" policy with respect to discouraging the use of detergents, citing the fact that other products, some chemicals for example, also contain phosphorus and contribute to the eutrophication problem. Banning detergents, therefore, will not necessarily cure the problem. Moreover, not all bodies of water are equally affected by introducing phosphate detergents into them. For example, fast moving streams may be relatively unharmed.

The uncertainty over how to deal effectively with the problem of detergents has led to some confusion in policy statements coming from Washington. Hard-line approaches in one government agency may be contradicted by a softer stance in another agency. The effect on the consumer may have been accurately described by a newspaper headline on the subject: "Detergents: What's a Mother to Do?"[7]

Confusion over appropriate government policy concerning environmental questions is not limited to detergents. The confusion stems from several sources.[8] First is the technical confusion noted in the detergents' case. We are simply uncertain what the facts are and what constitutes a legitimate hazard. Second, the existence of competing and overlapping governmental jurisdictions muddies the waters. Agencies at the city, county, state, and federal levels are dealing with environmental matters, and their approaches and standards do not always coincide. Confounding that problem is the fact that governmental standards present a moving target. Today's standards may give way to tougher requirements tomorrow. Finally, the interrelatedness of the pollution evil creates problems of its own. Example: coal-fired electric generating plants use precipitators to reduce the emission of soot and fly ash from their smokestacks. These devices operate by using the sulphur in coal to attract an electrical charge that precipitates the solids in the stack gases. Using coal with low sulphur content can reduce the emission of noxious sulphur dioxide but it renders precipitators ineffective. Furthermore, low sulphur coal is in short supply and is higher priced than ordinary steam coal. The use of nuclear power plants resolves the air pollution problems but creates thermal pollution problems from the discharge of condensing water into streams and lakes adjacent to the power plants.

Coordination of environmental matters through the Environmental Protection Agency may reduce confusion at the federal level, but the problem of coordinating activities at other governmental levels still would exist. Developing products and production processes under the handicaps of enforcement confusion, gaps in our technical knowledge

---

[7] For a good review of the conflicting public policy stands, see "Detergents: What's a Mother to Do?", *Wall Street Journal,* October 22, 1971, p. 8.

[8] "Companies Complain that Pollution Laws Conflict, Change Often," *Wall Street Journal,* December 23, 1970, p. 1.

of the subject, and shifting standards creates a particularly challenging environment in which business firms will operate in the coming years.

PRODUCT DIFFERENTIATION AND BRANDING   Marketing critics deplore the use of brand labeling and product differentiation for several reasons. They see some product differentiation as an attempt—with the aid of advertising—to make minor product differences appear major. Producers of major durables—such as automobiles—often come under attack. Critics point to the use of nonutilitarian "frills" as ways to confuse the buyer and add unnecessarily to the cost of the product. They see advertising as the agent that magnifies the importance of minor differences and as another contributor to higher costs. Branding receives similar criticism. Producers are seen to engage in it to increase market power by establishing customer loyalty for their brands over others.

To some extent, producers view product differentiation and branding similarly. Marketing texts extol branding and differentiation as tools in the marketer's profit-maximizing kit. But they also ascribe to these measures features which benefit the consumer and which critics ignore. Among product differentiation's alleged advantages to the consumer are the opportunities it provides for greater variety and choice, for improved product quality, and for better services including warranties.[9]

Trademarks, as adjuncts to product differentiation, date back to the medieval period. Craftsmen used marks to distinguish the output of particular guilds as a way to police the quality of their workmanship. Thus, guild members viewed the use of marks as a liability since, with their use, workers could not escape responsibility. Later, when guilds sold goods in nonlocal markets, trademarks developed a new function of assuring the buyer of product quality. The use of trademarks flourished in this way from the 15th to the 17th century, especially in the clothing and cutlery trades.[10]

Factories competing with the guilds also used product differentiation. As markets expanded following the medieval period, individual factory operators sought to compete with guild merchants by offering distinctive (differentiated) products to win consumer favor. Emphasis centered on maintaining quality to combat the quality image of guild-produced

[9] O. J. Firestone, *The Economic Implications of Advertising* (London: Methuen, 1967), p. 83.
[10] Neil H. Borden, *The Economic Effects of Advertising,* pp. 22–23.

goods. Not until much later, under the pressure of competition, did sellers consciously create minor product differences to develop "selling points"—the alleged practice that now attracts criticism.

Branding is not necessarily limited to capitalist societies. Theodore Levitt reports on the Russians' use of trademarks to correct a problem in their television industry.[11] Russian TV manufacturers found sales lagging. Several factories produced identical 17-inch sets but the output of one was inferior to the others. Buyers, however, tended to shun purchases of *all* sets of this type, not knowing which sets were defective. Inventories built up. This condition led to the use of trademarks to identify brands. Started as a convenience to planners, the trademark became a buying aid for the consumer. In this instance, brand recognition promoted economic welfare in two ways: by aiding the buying process and by singling out efficient producers for reward and exposing producers of shoddy goods.

Defenders of branding argue that it has the same beneficial effects in the United States' market-oriented system. Its use assures consumers of quality. But, the critics ask, why pay for the enormous advertising necessary to provide brand-name recognition? Why not emphasize the use of private, nonadvertised brands that afford excellent bargains in many lines of consumer goods? The marketer responds by noting that private branding depends upon the prior successful acceptance of advertised brands that stand as buying reference points.

To the charge that product differentiation harms the consumer by deceiving him into thinking that nominal product differences are significant, the defender of marketing answers that, far from harming him, it can serve him. How? By permitting producers to fashion products that meet consumer's *precise* needs. Differentiation recognizes that needs and desires among consumers vary with respect to colors, sizes, features, and psychological significance of products. The absence of product differentiation is product homogeneity. Is this, the marketer asks, an acceptable alternative?

The critic, however, wants less to dispense with product differentiation than to correct its abuses—the use of deceptive packaging to create the illusion of size, the nonfunctional gadget adorning a new model which distinguishes it from the old, the drumbeat of advertising which tries to distinguish one brand from its essentially identical competitor.

---

[11] Theodore Levitt, "Branding on Trial," *Harvard Business Review* (March–April 1966), pp. 113–115.

As the critic sees it, this behavior both confounds the consumer and adds to the cost of goods he purchases without providing corresponding benefits.

PLANNED PRODUCT OBSOLESCENCE   Recent years have seen the growing charge that continuing product changes by manufacturers are an attempt not to improve the consumer's welfare but to create sales through forced obsolescence of existing models. The charge is related to the criticism of product differentiation, only here the differentiation over time is seen not so much as a move to meet or beat competitors' offerings as it is an attempt to extend the product life cycle by continually obsolescing existing models. The automobile industry feels the full brunt of the charge of planned obsolescence, but other manufacturers—especially of durables and fashion goods—also come under attack.

Few argue against product developments that genuinely improve the quality and functional ability of products.[12] One need only recall earlier versions of automobiles, television sets, radios, airplanes, and a host of modern products to recognize the value of product development. The critics thus do not necessarily rail against all product change; rather they attack what they see as planned obsolescence. But how can we make a distinction? To do so might require probing the producer's mind to see what motivates the product changes. Presumably he hopes that enough consumers will view his new product offering as sufficiently attractive to warrant their purchase of it. If he changes a model to induce sales, and buyers are unimpressed, the producer suffers.

So-called planned obsolescence is not necessarily confined to manufacturers. Most inventors and developers of new processes usually create obsolescence of something previously developed. The development of the transistor rendered vacuum tubes in some uses obsolete, and one could argue that the outcome was "planned." Some of the most vocal critics of planned obsolescence are economists who regularly cause editions of their best-selling economics text to become obsolete by publishing revised editions that closely resemble the original.

What is the cost of creating product obsolescence? It often results

[12] Increased concern for the quality of life raises the number of those who look with disfavor on a growing list of "improvements" which society formerly assumed to be civilized advancements.

in a waste of resources. The new edition of the economics text requires, for all practical purposes, the scrapping of previous editions, with its attendant waste. For some products—automobiles, for example—a secondhand market prolongs the useful life of obsoleted models until they reach the end of their functional life. For other products—some books, clothes, furniture—the used markets may offer only partially effective means of prolonging product life, and hence conserving resources.

Those who condemn planned obsolescence see a waste not only in obsoleted models but also in the resources used for "frills" that represent the differentiating features. Whatever form the waste takes, however, it results in the depletion of precious, nonrenewable resources. Thus the needs (whims?) of the current generation are satisfied at the expense of generations unborn. Furthermore, it is argued, in addition to being an *absolute* waste of resources, planned obsolescence results in a misallocation of resources. This is essentially the Galbraithian "Affluent Society" thesis already examined—the issue of tail fins versus public parks.

The waste-of-resources argument is hard for marketers to rebut in view of the demonstrably threatened exhaustion of certain natural resources in the foreseeable future, and the force of arguments concerning pollution and ecological imbalance.

As a matter of public policy and necessity during World War II, the United States resolved the problem of wasting resources on "frills" by decreeing their abandonment. Thus, trousers were cuffless and books were printed without large margins. Presumably we could institute a similar policy to conserve resources, but the absence of a perceived emergency might make it unworkable. Alternatively the federal government might impose sanctions on producers who waste resources through the use of "unnecessary" product obsolescence, but here, too, implementation may be next to impossible without putting the economy in a straightjacket. A consumers' revolt against frequent and insignificant model changes probably holds the best hope for reducing the use of planned obsolescence. The success of the Volkswagen in competition with Detroit's constantly changing models augurs well for the success of this alternative solution. Clarence Walton raises an interesting question that closes this discussion. He asks whether we can be sure that the consumer is better off by having a choice of a television set lasting five years and one, at twice the price, lasting fifteen years (which the consumer, rationally, selects), in view of the genuine product improvement that can occur in the interim.[13] He also wonders whether building things to last forever is necessarily good, citing the ugly, solid homes on Riverside Drive in New York as case examples arguing for impermanence.[14]

TRUTH IN PACKAGING   A part of the so-called Truth-in-Packaging Act (Fair Packaging and Labeling Act), passed in 1966, reads: "Informed consumers are essential to the fair and efficient functioning of a free market economy. Packages and their labels should enable consumers to obtain accurate information as to the quantity of the contents and should facilitate value comparisons."[15] It is the failure of many packages and labels adequately to inform consumers that led to passage of the law. Extensive Congressional hearings revealed the depth and character of consumers' displeasure with packaging practices. Congressman Leonard Farbstein cited the most frequently mentioned abuses.

"1. The widespread lack of uniformity in the location of the information, such as the quantity statement, that is required by law to appear on the packages.

2. The lack of reasonable and efficient standardization of package sizes.

3. The use of such misleading qualifying terms as 'jumbo,' 'giant,' 'full,' and others.

4. The smallness of type and the lack of contrast in colors.

5. The use of packages and containers in designs that make the package appear to be larger than its actual contents justify.

6. The practice of marking a package 'cents-off' when all too frequently such offers represent no actual price reductions."[16]

Widely quoted in support of the bill, during debate prior to its passage

[13] Clarence C. Walton, "Ethical Theory, Societal Expectations and Marketing Practices," in William D. Stevens (ed.), *The Social Responsibilities of Marketing,* Proceedings of Winter Conference, American Marketing Association, December 1961, p. 22.
[14] Ibid., p. 22.
[15] Public Law 89-755, 89th Congress, p. 1296.
[16] U.S. House of Representatives, Committee on Interstate and Foreign Commerce, *Hearings on Fair Packaging and Labeling,* 89th Congress, 2nd Session, 1966, p. 20.

was research conducted by Professor Monroe Friedman, a psychologist from Eastern Michigan University. He asked 33 young women college graduates to shop for 20 supermarket items. Each was instructed to seek out the cheapest brand. This stricture resulted in their spending three times longer to shop than usual. The research revealed that 43% of the purchase decisions involved buying other than the cheapest brand. Not one shopper, for example, bought the lowest price detergent. Overall, the women spent 9% more than they should have had they selected the best bargains.[17] The inference that one presumably should draw from the results was that if college-educated women could not discern values from packages and labels taking extra time and care, the average buyer is hopelessly handicapped.

Opposition to the bill centered on the deleterious effects it might have on competition. D. Beryl Maneschewitz argued that "Standardized packages can lead to standardized products and standardized quality, and thereby limit the range of choice of the purchasing public. Under such conditions, marketing innovation and competition as well cannot help but suffer."[18] It is hard to understand why standardized packages necessarily lead to standardized products. Couldn't one argue that standardization would lead to *more* and not less competition since evidence points to standardized products being subjected to more price competition than differentiated ones? For example, regulations sponsored by the National Bureau of Standards governed package sizes for the dairy industry before passage of Truth-in-Packaging. They have led to the absence of odd-ounce containers for dairy products. Dairies limit themselves to pints, quarts, gallons, and so on; yet the industry exhibits as much price competition as can be expected from one bound by restrictive state laws. Restricting package sizes also has not inhibited the introduction of new products.

The Fair Packaging and Labeling Act provides that:

1. Goods must bear labels identifying the product, and the name and place of business of the manufacturer.

2. The quantity of a package's contents (weight, measure, or count) must be stated on labels in conspicuous type. Ingredients must be listed in order of their proportion.

3. Authority to issue regulations under the act rests with the F.D.A. and F.T.C., which can exempt products from coverage of the act

17 Ibid., p. 20.
18 Ibid., p. 80.

if its provisions are impractical or unnecessary for the consumer's protection. These agencies may also issue regulations concerning placement of printed matter relating to "cents off" on labels and to "nonfunctional slack-fill of packages."

4. If certain products spawn a proliferation of package sizes, the Secretary of Commerce may seek the establishment of voluntary product size standards from manufacturers.

5. Labels must bear the "common or usual" name of the product.

Both foes and advocates of the law find fault with its final version. Ralph Nader has labeled Truth-in-Packaging "the most deceptive package of all." His objection stems from the voluntary mechanism for reducing the number of package sizes. Even in the absence of mandatory controls, by mid-1968, a number of industries had agreed to eliminate many package sizes. Cereal packages had been cut from 33 to 16, detergents from 24 to 6, toothpaste from 57 to 5.

Others argue that previously existing F.T.C. rulings prohibited practices that the new law sought to abolish—especially with respect to the use of slack-filled packages and deceptive labeling.[19] The new law, however, moves beyond the prevention of deception, which may be hard to prove, but permits the setting of standards that will improve the buyer's knowledge of what he purchases.

Analysts who have studied marketing practices of low-income buyers see a drawback to the *conception* of Truth-in-Packaging. The criticism applies equally well to Truth-in-Lending legislation which is discussed below. Both laws assume the shopper has certain characteristics:

1. She shops around for good buys.

2. She is able to judge and therefore, secure, the best values.

3. She is aware of her legal rights and is willing to use legal remedies to protect herself.[20]

Truth-in-Packaging is informational legislation. It assumes that the average shopper lacks sufficient information to make intelligent buying decisions. For the law to be effective it must assume that shoppers will

[19] See, for example, "The Truth About Truth-in-Packaging," *Nation's Business* (October 1966), p. 75.

[20] For a discussion of these points, see Eric Schnapper, "Consumer Legislation and the Poor," in Aaker and Day (eds.), op. cit., p. 341.

use the new information available to them to improve the buying process. Unfortunately many low-income buyers—and others as well —lack the three characteristics listed above which would enable them to take advantage of the law's passage.

This objection raises a philosophical question concerning the two informational bills just mentioned as well as other proposed consumerism measures. To what extent should the state take action to provide information that will make for more rational buying decisions? Should it act even though the majority of buyers fail to use it? How can one balance the potential gain to those who use (and presumably profit by) it against the alleged disadvantages—for example, stifled competition, bureaucratic red tape, etc.? Few people would disagree that the public deserves protection from deception and access to information that will improve buying decisions. Dispute rages over the extent of the information that shoppers can effectively use, whether the government ought to mandate its dissemination and whether, if the demand is sufficient, a free market system cannot adequately provide for it. The reader might consider these questions and try to reach a reasoned position.

Although Truth-in-Packaging is a product-oriented issue, it also has informational aspects, as mentioned. Other consumer issues are more directly concerned with information and promotion.

INFORMATION AND PROMOTION □ The efficient functioning of a free market system depends upon the availability of adequate market information. Making rational buying decisions where choice is available requires that shoppers have access to accurate product information, and knowledge of terms and conditions of sales. Much of the current interest in consumerism centers on the improvement in the quality and amount of information available to the consumer. Attention also focuses on various promotional devices and procedures on the grounds that promotion may create distortions that confound the buying process. This section studies some of the issues in this area that have captured the attention of consumer advocates.

TRUTH-IN-LENDING   Usury and objections to it have an ancient lineage. In the Middle Ages the Church took a strong stand against the practice. The moneylender has always been suspect, and continual measures have been taken to limit the interest he may charge on loans. The laws in many states today control usury through statutory maxima of interest rates.

In recent years consumer protection in this area has taken a new direction. The so-called Truth-in-Lending law seeks to protect consumer interests by providing full disclosure of interest rates and credit terms on the premise that disclosure lets the consumer protect himself from credit abuse. Passed in 1968, the Consumer Credit Protection Act (the official title) provides for disclosure of: the annual rate of interest of all finance charges on credit transactions, the method of determining the finance charge, conditions under which additional charges may be imposed, and the minimum periodic payment that may be required.[21] Thus, when a credit transaction specifies interest at the rate of 1½% a month it must also state the annual rate of 18%. An installment payment schedule of $X a month must be accompanied by a statement indicating the annual interest rate that contributes to the schedule.

How effective is the law in accomplishing its purpose? A Federal Reserve Board survey in 1970 found 21% of new car buyers with installment loans were unaware of the interest rate charged them, as were 42% of new furniture buyers.[22] Thirty-five percent of the car buyers estimated the interest charges much too low (less than 7% when they were nearly double that figure). The Federal Reserve Board also found a high rate of compliance with the law. The discouraging results indicate, therefore, not abuse of the law by creditors but either a failure of borrowers to remember the interest rates or their failure to learn the rates when they arranged for credit. An encouraging note is an F.R.B. finding that this survey showed a "significant improvement" in consumers' awareness of interest charges compared to results of a survey taken just prior to the act's passage.[23]

Homer Kripke also finds Truth-in-Lending ineffective.[24] He doubts the efficacy of providing low-income shoppers with information on financing. He sees the law using middle-class solutions (disclosure) to a low-income class problem. He cites evidence in the bill's hearings that many credit users failed to realize that they had to pay finance charges even though they signed documents that indicated the charges. Furthermore, he sees many low-income buyers trapped into using credit because of their low or nonexistent cash resources. They may realize full

---

[21] Some of these specific requirements come from Federal Reserve Board regulations provided by the act and not directly from the wording of the act itself.

[22] "Loan Rates Confound Consumers," *Orlando Sentinel,* February 7, 1971, p. 17-A.

[23] Ibid.

[24] Homer Kripke, "Gesture and Reality in Consumer Credit Reform," in Aaker and Day (eds.), op. cit., pp. 163–168.

well the crushing credit burden that they undertake but remain power-
less to overcome it. Kripke complains also that the Consumer Credit
Protection Act fails to cover fraud and deception in selling—a more
serious problem as he sees it.

The evidence of the effectiveness of Truth-in-Lending is too scanty
to indicate its success in dealing with credit abuses. As with Truth-in-
Packing—and other proposals discussed below—its success depends
upon the use by consumers of the information that it provides. Kripke
has perceived what may be a bitter irony—that those with low incomes
who most need the law's protection may benefit little; instead the gains,
if any, may accrue to those with less need and more income.

TRUTH-IN-ADVERTISING   Advertising can inform. It also has the
ability to deceive. Marketing's critics view the deception with alarm and
seek ways to eliminate or curtail it. The pressure for reform comes at a
time when the consumer's job has become increasingly difficult. She
faces a bewildering array of new and competing products. Some
are rather complex. The media subject her to a barrage of messages
from competing sellers which, rather than informing the buyer, may
confuse her. Confronted with claims and counterclaims, she must also
guard against being misled by outright deception and misstatement of
fact. The Federal Trade Commission helps to police the situation, but
the problem's enormous size makes effective control difficult.

Here again Nader's Center for Study of Responsive Law has spear-
headed a reform movement. A task force monitored advertisements in
the print and broadcast media in the District of Columbia for a period
of time and recorded the exaggerated and deceptive claims that they
observed.[25] Deception took the following forms.

1. Claims based on supposed clinical evidence with no documentation of the claims. For example, "Nytol dissolves twice as fast
   as the other leading sleep tablets," "a survey of hospital patients showed: two Excedrin more effective in the relief of pain
   than twice as many aspirin."

2. Claims of product features that presumably benefit the consumer without showing *specifically* what form the benefit takes.
   For example, "Lavoris scrubs your breath clean."

3. "Dangling comparatives—implied comparisons for which the

[25] Ralph Nader and Aileen Adams, Petition for Trade Regulation Rule Proceed-
ing and Issuance of Enforcement Policies before Federal Trade Commission.

basis of the comparison is not revealed." For example, Dow's oven cleaner has "33% more power," Armour bacon "gives you a little more because it shrinks a little less."

4. Commercials showing superior results for a product when used in a nonnormal fashion. For example, Schick showing 17 men getting a close shave from one blade within a short period of time—hardly the usual practice.

Nader and several other consumer groups have proposed trade regulations to help correct the abuses that they observed. They would require national advertisers to file with the Federal Trade Commission information that would substantiate their claims. Companies would make the data available *prior* to the ads' publication. The regulations would require local and regional advertisers to make the substantiating information available upon request by the F.T.C. or the public.

In June 1971, the F.T.C. adopted a limited version of these suggestions by ordering industries "to file data in support of claims involving the safety, performance, efficacy, quality, and comparative prices of advertised products,"[26] on an industry-by-industry basis, every three months. The files will be made available to the public. The first order covered the automobile industry. Firms will have 60 days to substantiate claims questioned by the F.T.C.

The F.T.C.'s announced rationale for the order was threefold: (1) public disclosure would help consumers make more rational decisions; (2) the availability of information would improve competition by permitting firms to question rival's claims; and (3) companies, realizing the need for substantiating claims and subjecting them to public scrutiny, would be more sure of their facts before claiming special attributes for their products.[27] In opposition to the regulation, it is claimed that having to substantiate claims will cause the consumer to receive less, not more, information as sellers become more cautious.[28]

The F.T.C. order falls short of Nader's (and others') suggestion, which called for *all* claims to be substantiated and not just those challenged by the commission. The commission, on the other hand, hopes that industry, as a result of its move, will police itself more effectively

[26] "F.T.C. to Order Industries to Substantiate Their Ads," *New York Times,* June 11, 1971, p. 1.

[27] Ibid., p. 17.

[28] "F.T.C. to Require Public Proof of Ad Claims," *Wall Street Journal,* June 11, 1971, p. 2.

than before. Meanwhile, a bill—the Truth-in-Advertising Act—would make illegal the advertising of products for which adequate documentation of claims is unavailable. The F.T.C. regulation may postpone this type of legislation pending a review of the regulation's effectiveness.

An interesting development is the F.T.C. orders in 1971 requiring firms charged with deceptive advertising to confess their alleged sins in subsequent advertisements. Thus Profile bread, which advertises its slimming properties, was ordered to spend at least 25% of its ad expenditures for one year announcing that Profile bread is not effective for weight reduction. The F.T.C. also charged Coca Cola and Standard Oil of California with deceptive advertising and ordered them to admit their alleged misrepresentations in future ads.[29] These two companies protested the order and have taken the cases to court, but the ITT Continental Baking Co., Profile's manufacturer, has agreed to a consent order.

The F.T.C.'s approach to regulating advertising views the consumer as an economic man who makes purchase decisions rationally on the basis of objective data. But, Dorothy Cohen argues, the buyer is as much a behavioral man as he is an economic man.[30] Full disclosure helps to protect economic man and improve his buying performance, but it is inadequate. Opinion leaders, brand loyalty and brand images, social group norms, and other noneconomic factors may be as important as objective data in regulating buyer behavior. Cohen reminds us also that people selectively accept information, blocking some messages and letting others filter through. Habits, biases, attitudes, and social relationships may influence one's receptivity to consumer information as much as one's intelligence does. Thus, a policy that is based on disclosure of objective facts and ignores subjective considerations may be ineffective.

There is another problem, even when objective information is made available. "Technological change is so rapid that the consumer who bothers to learn about a commodity or a service soon finds his knowledge obsolete. In addition, many improvements in quality and performance are below the threshold of perception, and imaginative marketing often makes rational choice even more of a problem."[31]

[29] Federal Trade Commission, *News Summary,* November 1, 1970, and August 1971.

[30] Dorothy Cohen, "The Federal Trade Commission and the Regulation of Advertising in the Consumer Interest," *Journal of Marketing* (January 1969), pp. 40–44.

[31] *Consumer Issues '66,* A Report Prepared by the Consumer Advisory Council

UNIT PRICING   The billions of dollars spent on grocery shopping create an enormous potential for improvement from consumer-oriented reforms. Two of these reforms which command considerable interest are unit pricing and open-code dating of food products.

Those pleading for reform of grocery store pricing charge that the shopper faces an impossible task in calculating values correctly and quickly. Faced with a proliferation of products, package sizes, and price offerings, the average shopper is hard-pressed to determine whether he makes the best buys. Which is the better buy: an 8¼-ounce can of pineapple for 19¢ or the 13¼-ounce size for 30¢?

Unit pricing is suggested as a partial solution to this dilemma. It calls for dual pricing of grocery products: one price for the full package or can, the other on a price per unit (e.g., ounce) basis. The unit measurement gives the shopper a standard for comparing competitive product prices. Thus, in the foregoing example, the unit prices for the two sizes respectively would be 2.30¢ and 2.27¢ per ounce.

One-fifth of all United States supermarkets were reported using unit pricing in 1970.[32] Approximately one-half of the consumers in a survey taken then recognized and understood the operation of unit pricing, but those standing to profit most from its use—minority groups and the aged—understood it the least. Most of those who understood unit pricing liked it and two-thirds of them used it. But this study cites several disadvantages. The costs of introducing and maintaining unit pricing are relatively high in grocery retailing, where margins are low. For example, Jewel Tea Co. estimated the cost per store of introducing unit pricing to be $1000.[33] Small, independent stores may suffer a special handicap since they are less able than large chain stores to absorb the additional expense. They face a dilemma—unable to afford the additional expense, but subject to a competitive disadvantage if they do not. There may also be a problem keeping price labels up to date.

Jewel Tea Co., one of the early users of unit pricing, reached similar conclusions based on their early experience. After seven months of operation, almost half of their customers had used unit pricing at least once; 30% used it on a regular basis; 41% considered it worthwhile.

(Washington, D.C.: U.S. Government Printing Office, 1966), p. 6, quoted in Cohen, ibid.

[32] John S. Coulson, " 'New Consumerists' Breed Will Fade Away," *The Marketing News,* Mid-June, 1971, p. 5.

[33] "Unit Pricing Chalks Up Some Surprises," *Business Week,* October 31, 1970, p. 80.

They too found it used more by high-income than by low-income shop-pers. A particular problem involved pricing concentrated products (e.g., frozen orange juice) with different dilution ratios. Should the unit price apply to the diluted or undiluted quantity? A similar problem arises with canned fruits and vegetables having different moisture contents.

Massachusetts is the first state to have passed a unit pricing law. It permits a Consumers Council to decide, after conducting hearings, which products will be unit priced. New York City also requires unit pricing. At the federal level, a unit pricing bill has been proposed but has not been acted on. As with many other consumerism issues, little evidence exists to show the extent of popular support for legislative action covering the matter.

Although we have treated the consumerism issues separately, many of them are interrelated. The unit pricing and truth-in-packaging issues illustrate the point. Unit pricing seeks to standardize prices to reduce confusion over unit values. But part of the existing confusion over prices stems from deceptive packaging. Truth-in-packaging will not simul-taneously solve the problem that unit pricing seeks to alleviate, but it works toward the same end.

OPEN-CODE DATING   Most packaged food products bear a code indicating a date that measures the product's freshness. The average consumer would have to be an amateur cryptographer to decipher the many codes in use. They are designed for use by the distributors and manufacturers. In recent years consumers have sought to change the coding system to improve their knowledge of product freshness. A survey of consumers found that those citing open-code dating as a needed consumer reform outnumbered those favoring unit pricing more than two to one (49% vs. 23%).

Jewel Tea Co. claims to have been the first retailer to introduce open dating in July 1970.[34] Although no data exist on the dollar volume of food products sold with open-code dating, increasing numbers of food chains and manufacturers have begun the practice, if only experimen-tally. Six months after Jewel Tea began the practice, approximately 30 companies were open dating.[35]

Most manufacturers, understandably, prefer coded dating. It permits them to control quality without letting consumers sort out new from older merchandise. Manufacturers complain that earlier dated merchandise

[34] "Chains Woo with Open Dating," *Business Week*, January 16, 1971, p. 48.
[35] Ibid.

may be of acceptable quality, yet consumers choose fresher products when given a choice. This presents the manufacturer with unsold inventory problems. Retailers suffer the same handicap. Shoppers may buy 5-day-old eggs and leave 10-day-old eggs unsold even though eggs should remain fresh for 15 days.

Open-code dating creates additional problems. What date should be used? Should it be the date when it was manufactured, the date beyond which one should not eat the product, the date when the product should leave the shelf and make way for fresher products, or the date when its nutritional value begins to decline? Frozen foods create another problem. If improperly handled by the customer they can spoil before the code's expiration date. Is the company liable for loss in this event?

Although the survey cited above found consumers strongly favoring open dating, many fail to use it when it is made available to them.[36] Even if many ignore it, consumers should benefit from the pressure on retailers to be alert to the need for product freshness.

PROMOTIONAL GAMES   Marketers use a number of promotional devices for generating sales, especially for recently introduced or mature products. A favorite device in recent years is the promotional game which has been heavily used by gasoline companies and grocery chains. Increasing consumer complaints concerning the games' operations have led to several Congressional and state legislative hearings.

Testimony in the Congressional hearings revealed several forms of deception in the gas station games. The games varied among companies but each offered contestants a galaxy of prizes—some substantial, most inexpensive—for winning the contest (in some kind of game format). Most of the deception involved leading participants to believe that their chances of winning—especially large prizes—were greater than was actually possible. Deception includes:

•   Selecting specific stations or individuals to receive major prizes. For example, testimony reveals that an oil company official arranged for two of a state's 500 stations to receive the top prizes. Thus customers of the remaining 498 stations were deceived into thinking that they could win a top prize that was unavailable to them.

•   Timing of winners to create the impression that the odds of winning were large. Companies "seeded" contest boxes to insure more winners in the contest's early weeks to enhance publicity.

[36] Ibid., p. 51.

• Favoring special customers with winning tickets, or employees appropriating winning tickets for themselves. The hearings uncovered evidence of gas station's employees' ingenuity in determining winning packets or tickets. One not-so-ingenious effort involved employees finding that winning and nonwinning tickets came in separate envelopes!

• Stating false odds of winning.

Investigation of supermarket games revealed an almost identical pattern. The Federal Trade Commission has taken action to reduce or eliminate the games' abuses although adverse publicity seems temporarily to have diminished their use. Abuse of promotional devices like games and contests is typical of unfair trade practices which the F.T.C. tries to combat through administrative action. It has used this authority to provide participants of games and contests with more information about their chances of winning.

In 1971, there was an increase in F.T.C. activity to protect the consumer in several ways, but aside from enforcing the Wheeler-Lea Act, which deals with misleading advertising, most F.T.C. enforcement protects businesses from the effect of unfair trade practices and anticompetitive behavior of other businesses.

SELLING PRACTICES □ The salesman has taken more than his share of criticism. Whether selling attracts more charlatans and slick operators than other occupations is unknown. People seem to think so since selling as an occupation traditionally ranks low in prestige and salesmen often are the butt of jokes.

Objections to salesmen and their tactics run the gamut from displeasure with high pressure tactics at one extreme to outright fraud at the other. Public policy probably cannot deal with the former; existing law covers the latter. Concern here lies less with salesmen's shortcomings and more with selling *procedures,* with which public policy might deal. Two practices are singled out for further study: a brief look at negative option selling, and door-to-door selling, which commands more attention.

NEGATIVE OPTION SELLING Ten million subscribers pay $250 million a year for negative option purchases.[37] Under this arrangement,

[37] John D. Morris, "Apathy Perils U.S. Plan to Ban 'Negative Option' Sales Method," *New York Times,* November 23, 1970, p. 32.

the buyer agrees to accept and pay for merchandise unless he rejects it within a specified period of time. Record companies and book publishers account for most sales of this type. A Federal Trade Commission hearing revealed a number of abuses of the system including inadequate time for subscribers to return negative option cards, insufficient advance information on how the plans operate, the delivery of unwanted merchandise in place of what subscribers ordered, the use of deception in trying to collect on phony bills, and inadequate attention to customers' complaints. The commission also sees a fundamental drawback to negative option selling, in addition to specific abuses. They view the practice as playing on people's traits of forgetfulness and procrastination and exploiting their preoccupation with more pressing personal matters. Dr. Ernest van den Haag, a psychiatrist supporting the industry, counters this assertion. He thinks "subscribers may be aware of their own weaknesses and of their tendency to be diverted and to procrastinate, and they may subscribe as a result of their awareness. Thus they may cause themselves to do what the spirit is willing to do but what the flesh may be too weak to carry out."[38]

Hearings to consider regulations banning negative option selling as an unfair and deceptive trade practice created expected industry opposition but little public interest in the restriction. This absence of support may confirm Dr. van den Haag's position or may indicate that the alleged annoyance of negative option selling is insufficient to get many people excited about the issue.

DOOR-TO-DOOR SELLING   Door-to-door selling has been under attack for a number of years. Agitation for its control springs from two sources: disgruntled consumers who have been bilked by door-to-door salesmen or annoyed by the practice, and local retailers who resent the competition. Pressure from retailers has led, in some communities, to licensing requirements controlling the quality of people engaged in door-to-door selling. A more severe restriction is the so-called "Green River" ordinance which exists in many communities.[39] This type of ordinance forbids solicitation in the home without consent of the resident. Use of the ordinance may limit what some consumers regard as an objectionable sales procedure, but it also limits competition by eliminating competitors of established local retailers. Local retailers

---

[38] Ibid.

[39] In addition, five states regulate door-to-door sales practices ("Consumerism: A New and Growing Face in the Marketplace," (3rd ed.), Burson-Marsteller, p. 13).

usually provide the impetus for passage of these ordinances although companies practicing door-to-door selling have succeeded in limiting the spread of the restrictive ordinance.

Congress has studied several bills to extend restrictions on door-to-door selling. Unlike the "Green River" ordinance, they usually seek not to abolish door-to-door selling, but to curtail some of its objectionable features. A discussion of the provisions of one of these bills may provide a useful summary of public attitudes toward door-to-door selling.

The Door-to-Door Sales Act (which has never gotten out of committee) aims principally to provide buyers of merchandise sold door-to-door an opportunity to reconsider their purchases. It gives a buyer until midnight of the following business day to cancel his purchase, and requires the seller to pick up the unwanted goods and effect a refund within three business days of receipt of the order's cancellation.[40] The bill seeks to control what its author sees as objectionable features of door-to-door selling—the combination of high pressure and, often, unethical selling and the unsolicited character of the transaction, which call for the "cooling-off" feature. Unethical persuasion may take countless forms. Tricks of the trade include: "bait and switch tactics, bogus contests, the model home pitch, the free gifts and sample offer, the official inspector impersonation, the specially selected household gimmick, verbal promises or implications, phoney bargains, trick financing, guarantees not honored, materials misrepresented, misleading pictorial renderings, social pressures, exaggerated product performance and scare tactics."[41]

Opponents of this legislation to curb door-to-door selling object on several grounds.[42] They view it as discriminating against door-to-door selling without dealing with other forms of unethical selling. They also feel it penalizes an entire industry to correct the abuses of a minority. Moreover, they see a "cooling-off" period weakening the concept of a contract. Implying that door-to-door selling is a shady occupation will make it even harder, it is argued, to recruit reputable salesmen—thus exacerbating the problems that led to the legislation. Finally, opponents

---

[40] Six states already have this kind of legislation. The F.T.C. also proposed, in September 1970, a trade regulation rule which would give buyers of goods sold door-to-door three days in which to change their minds.

[41] Marvin A. Jolson, "Cooling Off the Door-to-Door Salesman," *Business and Economic Dimensions,* Bureau of Business and Economic Research, University of Florida, February 1971, p. 17.

[42] See Jolson, ibid., pp. 13–17.

would rather see legislation aimed at abuses of door-to-door selling rather than punitive legislation against the entire industry.

Neither legislation of this type nor a similar proposed F.T.C. trade regulation rule on door-to-door selling would deal with the invasion-of-privacy issue. Solicitation by a door-to-door salesman involves an unsolicited disturbance of one's privacy. Not unlike the unwanted guest, he intrudes into the household or, at a minimum, interrupts activity (or inactivity) long enough to have the doorbell answered. A similar problem exists with respect to telephone solicitation which remains pretty well unchecked. In both cases one may ask which right should be paramount: the right of sellers to ply their trade in a particular way or the right of citizens to protect themselves from unsolicited invasions of privacy by vendors? Limiting telephone and door-to-door solicitation does not rule out alternative ways of selling.

PRICING PRACTICES □ The stereotypical conception of the American economic system runs as follows: it is a free enterprise, capitalistic economy; competition lies at the heart of free enterprise; since freely fluctuating, market-determined prices form the cornerstone of competition, the American consumer reaps the benefits of vigorous price competition. Of course, this conception falls far short of reality. The United States has a mixed system, with active government influence and participation in many sectors of the economy mixed with free enterprise sectors exhibiting various degrees of competitive behavior. Some sectors witness vigorous price competition; in others, government or industry price-fixing arrangements nullify price competition.

The rationale for government intervention in price making is ambiguous. On the one hand government intervention seeks to maintain vigorous price competition; on the other it limits it. Its ambiguous posture undoubtedly reflects the conflicting pressures exerted on government by private interests. The result is a crazyquilt pattern of intervention which strengthens competition with the left hand and weakens it with the right. This section on pricing focuses on this ambivalent policy to see whether, on balance, government intervention in the price-making process benefits or hinders the consumer.

PROCONSUMER PRICING PROTECTION   Government intervention in the pricing process on the consumer's side takes four forms. All of the remaining government measures in this area—and there are many—aim to protect competitors from each other and in so doing constitute probusiness, anticonsumer measures. Of the four proconsumer measures, three are more or less permanent, embedded into law or court decisions; the fourth is an emergency remedy that protects consumers when conditions warrant its use.

The strongest protection that consumers may receive against unfair prices is a competitive economy. Often, however, sellers try to seal off markets and artificially raise prices through collusive price-fixing agreements. Fortunately for consumers, price fixing is a per se violation of the antitrust laws. Protection comes not from statutory language outlawing price rigging, but from court cases against the practice, which date back to the end of the 19th century. The rulings derive from authority in Section 1 of the Sherman Act, which outlaws "Every contract, combination in the form of trust or otherwise, or conspiracy, in restraint of trade or commerce among the several states. . . ." Few would claim that antitrust enforcement of price fixing eliminates the practice from the American business scene. In fact, approximately two-thirds of the cases handled by the Antitrust Division of the Justice Department involve price fixing.[43] Nonetheless, it is bound to be a deterrent, especially in the aftermath of such highly publicized price fixing cases as the electrical equipment conspiracy in the early 1960s in which several top company officials served prison terms for their roles in the arrangement.

Consumer price protection also flows from the Wheeler-Lea Act of 1938, which amends Section 5 of the Federal Trade Commission Act to prohibit "unfair or deceptive acts or practices in commerce." The law applies to deception of several kinds including deceptive pricing practices. Price deception usually involves offering the consumer a better price deal than he actually receives. Fictitious reductions from inflated "original" prices are a typical case. The F.T.C. has issued "Guides against Fictitious Pricing" which spells out guidelines to prevent such an abuse. For industries generating many deceptive pricing complaints the commission publishes special regulations to limit deception in the consumer's interest.

The third area of government intervention to maintain fair pricing occurs in public utility regulation. The monopolistic character of most utilities dictates the control of their pricing power by regulatory agencies. Control rests with state or federal commissions depending on the geographical scope of the utilities' operations.

Government price controls and freezes represent the fourth type of

---

[43] Marshall C. Howard, *Legal Aspects of Marketing* (New York: McGraw-Hill, 1964), p. 28.

intervention on behalf of the consumer. This authority is generally used in emergency wartime situations to control threatened or actual price inflation. Thus World Wars I and II and the Korean conflict witnessed federal price controls that lasted through the emergency period. President Nixon's 90-day wage and price freeze, introduced in August 1971, sought to cope with a similar problem but in a modified peacetime environment.[44] Each of our wartime experiences with controls—especially the 1971 freeze—points up an interesting aspect of our attitude toward inflation protection. Over the long run, the American economy has experienced an increase in the average price level. There have been brief periods of sharp increase and, at times, reductions in the general level of prices, but the overall pattern of prices has been gradually upward. Public pressure to control prices is virtually nonexistent when the uptrend is gradual; it is only when accelerated inflation threatens or exists that public opinion swings toward support for controls. Whether a consumer suffers from price inflation depends largely on his ability to increase his income correspondingly. The enormous administrative burden of price controls and the rigidities in the economic system that they create are enough to discourage their use except in emergencies even though some consumers suffer inequities.[45]

PROBUSINESS PRICING PROTECTION The foregoing measures provide formidable consumer protection from unfair and anticompetitive pricing. But the pressure of special business interests has also created an impressive umbrella of anticompetitive devices that shelter sellers from the full impact of market forces. What follows is a brief account of some of these measures.

In some instances government intervention on behalf of sellers has an indirect rather than direct effect on prices. However, the impact is no less real. Examples are tariffs and quotas that discourage competition from foreign producers and reduce pressure on domestic producers to lower prices. No industry has done a more effective job to regulate competition by controlling supply than the petroleum industry. Oil import quotas limit supplies from abroad. State proration laws plus the Interstate Oil Compact effectively control domestic output. Matching

---

[44] One is hard-pressed to correctly categorize the American economy in mid-1971 as a wartime or peacetime economy.

[45] A quibbler might suggest that presidential exhortation is a fifth protection against price inequities. President Kennedy's successful effort to roll back steel prices in 1962 is a case in point. These efforts are very spasmodic and represent brief forays in the price battle rather than full-fledged and longer lasting protection.

supply to changing demand levels keeps control of the market price level in the producers' hands rather than letting it be determined by the vagaries of the marketplace. The system fails to prevent such aberrations as gasoline price wars, but it efficiently limits downward pressure on the *average* realization for all petroleum products.

Many states have enacted a variety of laws to curtail price cutting. These include:

1. Fair trade laws that permit contracts requiring retailers to charge a price no lower than a prescribed level.

2. Minimum markup laws ("Unfair Practices" Acts) designed principally to eliminate the use of "loss leaders." Almost two-thirds of the states at one time had passed laws of this type, but in a number of instances the courts have ruled against them. They also have invalidated fair trade laws.

3. State laws regulating the sale of specific commodities such as milk or liquor. These laws vary from state to state where they exist, but the intent and effect are pretty much the same. They protect the interests of the retailers (and, often, producers, especially in milk) from price competition. The protection usually shelters the small, higher cost retailers from the rigors of price cutting. Society suffers from a misallocation of resources; consumers lose the benefits of price competition.

Most of these three kinds of state laws trace their origin to the depression when the pressure was intense from beleaguered retailers for protection against the ravages of competition. At the federal level, protection during the same period took the form of agricultural price supports, the Robinson-Patman Act, and the National Industrial Recovery Act of 1933. Under the latter act, industry codes provided for minimum prices designed to alleviate ruinous competition. The act was declared unconstitutional in 1935, but the other two measures continue to exist even though conditions today are vastly different from those existing when they were introduced. The Robinson-Patman Act seeks to prevent certain kinds of price discrimination; however, the focus is on protection of sellers from one another rather than on protection of the consumer. As with the various protective state laws, it grew out of small retailers' complaints. They felt threatened by large distributors who had grown to prominence in the 1920s and 1930s.

This brief summary of the major government-supported devices to protect sellers from price competition gives some idea of the forces arrayed against the consumer who looks to a free market system for competitively determined prices. Fortunately for him, many of the state laws designed to stifle price competition have been ineffective, unenforceable, or rendered unconstitutional. This nullification has been especially true with the fair trade laws and minimum markup laws. Furthermore, not every state has enacted these protective laws. Where commodity control laws protecting cigarettes, milk, liquor, and so on exist, the consumer undoubtedly loses out to protected retailers. No one has studied the combined effect of these laws, but they artificially raise retail prices on goods with annual sales volume running into billions of dollars. One can assume that the effect on prices of the other restrictive measures is substantial but, here again, a precise estimate of the consumers' "losses" is unavailable and probably impossible to ascertain with any degree of precision.

It is tempting to think that the deterrent effect of the per se illegality of price fixing is adequate to compensate for these losses. But anyone who has been exposed to industrial price making and has had extensive contacts with marketing executives must be pessimistic. It is hard to imagine any action that would reap greater pecuniary benefits for the consumer than *consistently* vigorous antitrust enforcement at a scale far exceeding anything witnessed in the past. Political realism may nullify the possibility of such a reform, but that does not diminish its exciting possibilities.

□ DISCUSSION QUESTIONS □

1. How extensive should be the list of products protected by safety legislation? What criteria do you suggest using in establishing such a list?

2. The consumer often feels victimized by his inability to get warranty satisfaction from the retail dealer or manufacturer. It sometimes looks to him as though each is "passing the buck." To protect the consumer, should legislation provide that either the dealer or the manufacturer specifically be held accountable for warranty service?

Does this create any new problems? If you oppose legislation to remedy the problem, can you suggest a feasible alternative solution?

3. Check with a local drugstore on the number of toothpaste brands it carries. Are there too many, in your judgment? What criteria do you use in making this judgment? Does a large number of available brands for a product represent waste? Explain.

4. Think of a product that is periodically modified. Do these changes represent planned obsolescence? Are the changes wasteful? Deceptive?

5. Distinguish, if possible, between advertising "puffery" and deception. Can you cite specific examples of advertising that fall into each category?

6. Legislators and consumer advocates have proposed "Truth-in-Advertising" legislation that would require advertisers, prior to the ad's publication, to file information with the Federal Trade Commission substantiating their claims. Evaluate this proposal.

7. Is the consumer better or worse off with the existence of fair trade laws? Explain.

8. A company's Board of Directors represents its stockholders. What is your reaction to the suggestion that companies also have a Board of Consumers to represent consumers and the public in general?

6

Ghetto Marketing

Chapter 5 dealt with a host of consumerism issues; however, it ignored one issue that has commanded considerable interest and concern in recent years: the plight of ghetto residents. Their problems are numerous. The ones of special interest here are those involving interaction of ghetto residents with marketing institutions.

Ghetto marketing suffers from several alleged shortcomings. The charges are as follows.

- Ghetto residents pay too much for food and other products bought from local merchants.
- Unscrupulous merchants deceive ghetto shoppers with nefarious selling tactics, enslave them with extortionate credit terms.
- Control of retail institutions rests in the hands of outsiders who drain profits from the ghetto and who are unresponsive to ghetto inhabitants' needs. This condition calls for reform in the structure of business ownership.

As a social issue confronting marketing, ghetto marketing is sufficiently important to warrant separate treatment. This chapter exposes the problems, analyzes research results dealing with them, and discusses suggested remedies.

BACKGROUND ☐ The United States is characterized as an affluent society. Statistics on per capita income, consumption of durable goods, and the share of the world's wealth controlled by Americans confirm this statement. But the totals and averages mislead. They hide the existence of a large core of impoverished people to whom, for one reason or another, the dream of affluence is a myth. In fact, these Americans fall short of achieving even a minimal standard of living. More than two-thirds of the people with incomes below a poverty level are white, but the nonwhites, mostly Negroes, are more numerous than their share of the total population would warrant. Increasingly, these poor nonwhites concentrate in the ghettos in our major cities.

Ironically, concern for the welfare of ghetto inhabitants has increased as the number of persons with an income below the poverty line has decreased. In 1959, 39.5 million people had incomes below the poverty level; by 1970 this number had fallen to 25.5 million.[1] Several factors have led to the increased concern for the poor, not least of which is the incongruity of the presence of poverty in a land of plenty.

Ghetto residents spend a large share of their income in neighborhood stores; therefore, improvement in marketing conditions could alleviate their financial plight. This is especially true of food marketing, since it is estimated that the poor pay from 29 to 36% of their income on food, compared to 18% so spent by the average household.[2] To appraise the performance of marketing in the ghetto, we need to investigate prices there and compare them with prices outside of the ghetto. Of prime interest are food prices, and secondarily, are prices of nonfood items, particularly appliances.

GHETTO FOOD PRICES ☐ Do the poor pay more? This paraphrase of David Caplovitz's book title (*The Poor Pay More*) raises the central question. As the title implies, Caplovitz's study of ghetto families found that the poor, indeed, do pay more than nonghetto residents. He studied appliance prices. The evidence concerning ghetto food prices is uneven. We find some evidence that the poor pay more, some that they do not.

BUREAU OF LABOR STATISTICS STUDY[3]   The Bureau of Labor Statistics "found no significant differences in prices charged by food stores located in low-income areas versus those charged by stores in

[1] U.S. Department of Commerce, *Consumer Income,* Current Population Reports, May 7, 1971, p. 2.

[2] Figure for poor from David Caplovitz, "On the Value of Consumer Action Programs in the War on Poverty" prepared for Office of Economic Opportunity, March 8, 1966, and reported in *Consumer Problems of the Poor,* hearings before Special Studies Committee of Committee on Government Operations, House of Representatives, 90th Congress, 2nd Session, October 12, November 24 and 25, 1967, p. 5; average household figure from U.S. Department of Agriculture, "National Food Situation Report," November 17, 1967, also reported in *Consumer Problems of the Poor,* p. 5.

[3] U.S. Bureau of Labor Statistics, "A Study of Prices Charged in Food Stores Located in Low and Higher Income Areas of Six Large Cities," February 1966, reproduced in National Commission on Food Marketing, Technical Study No. 10, June 1966, pp. 122–144.

higher income areas, when the same types of stores (chains, large independents, small independents), the same qualities of foods, and the
same sizes of packages are compared."[4]

Thus the study found no evidence to support the allegation that ghetto
chain stores charge more than do chain operations in higher income
areas. They did find that small independents in both ghetto and nonghetto areas charge higher prices than either large independents or
chain stores. This condition handicaps ghetto dwellers since they, more
than high-income people, patronize small stores. Another handicap
facing the poor is their greater inclination to buy in small quantities.
This raises their food bill above what it would be if they were to purchase large, more economical sizes.

GOODMAN STUDY[5]   Charles S. Goodman analyzed prices paid by
Philadelphia ghetto residents in 1965, as well as their shopping behavior. He concluded that "the poor do *not* pay more,"[6] but, unlike the
B.L.S. report, Goodman did not compare ghetto prices with those outside of the ghetto. Thus the question arises: "They do not pay more
than whom?" He studied prices at twelve stores, equally divided among
supermarkets, medium-sized independents, and small convenience
stores. All of the supermarkets lay in a region extending one-half mile
from the boundary of the 160-acre residential area surveyed. The ghetto
shoppers were inclined to patronize either these supermarkets or three
of the four medium-sized independents whose prices were actually
below the supermarkets'. They tended to shun the local, higher-priced
stores, although the reasons for this (higher prices, poorer quality, limited variety) were not made clear. The important conclusions from the
pricing portion of Goodman's study are that his ghetto shoppers lacked
access to supermarkets in the immediate area, traveled some distance,
at least, to shop at lower-priced stores and, a corollary, perceived
price differences among the stores.

NEW YORK, WASHINGTON, D.C., AND ST. LOUIS STUDY[7]
Hearings of a House Subcommittee revealed generally higher prices
for food in the three cities studied in 1967. Market basket studies found

---

4 Ibid., p. 122.
5 Charles S. Goodman, "Do the Poor Pay More?" *Journal of Marketing* (January
1968), pp. 18–24.
6 Ibid., p. 23.
7 Reported in *Consumer Problems of the Poor*, op. cit., pp. 7–40.

prices from 6 to 15% higher in ghetto-area stores than in stores in higher income areas.[8]

The hearings checked into the allegation that ghetto chain stores raise prices on the dates ghetto residents receive welfare checks and food stamps. The market basket study for Washington, D.C., analyzed prices on welfare payday and two weeks earlier. Prices increased 9.5% between the two dates in ghetto chain stores and only 2.5% in stores outside of the ghetto.[9]

BROOKLYN STUDY   This study by the Consumer Action Program in 1967 compared prices for twenty items in three food chains in the Bedford-Stuyvesant and Flatbush areas of Brooklyn, representing low- and middle-income neighborhoods respectively. Prices in the ghetto stores ran from 3.5 to 6% above those in the higher income stores. The research also found support for the allegation of higher ghetto store prices around welfare payday. The average market basket value of the food at the three Flatbush stores fell a few pennies around the welfare payday but increased about 2.5% at the three Bedford-Stuyvesant stores.

The New York Council on Consumer Affairs, which studied prices both in chain and nonchain stores several days before welfare payday and on the payday, found price increases of "about 15%."[10]

WATTS STUDY[11]   The previous four studies reveal disturbing inconsistencies. The first two show that the poor may not pay more than others for food; the last two indicate that they do. Part of the problem stems from weaknesses in the research designs. Burton H. Marcus' Watts study remedies these defects to some extent.

Marcus studied prices on all available items included in the Consumer Price Index for a total of 49 stores in the Watts and Culver City areas of Greater Los Angeles. Watts is a recognized low-income area inhabited principally by nonwhites. Culver City is predominantly white and has a higher average income than Watts.

The Marcus study reveals a slightly lower average price level in the ghetto than in the nonghetto area. However, excluding meat and pro-

8 Ibid., p. 17.

9 Ibid.

10 Ibid., p. 20.

11 Burton H. Marcus, "Similarity of Ghetto and Nonghetto Food Costs," reproduced in David A. Aaker and George S. Day (eds.), *Consumerism: Search for the Consumer Interest,* pp. 382–389.

duce items, ghetto food prices were 4% higher. Since meat and produce quality may vary substantially, one may suspect that lower prices
for these items in the ghetto stores relate to their lower quality. Marcus'
findings are shown in Table 6–1.

TABLE 6–1 Percentage by Which Prices for Food Were Higher (Lower)
in Watts than Culver City

Product Group	Store Category		
	"Ma and Pa"	Supermarket	All Stores
Comparable product groups			
Cereal and bakery	6.0	1.3	3.7
Canned fruits and vegetables	9.0	0.3	4.6
Other foods	10.1	1.5	5.8
Noncomparable product groups			
Meat, poultry and fish	(11.5)	(3.2)	(7.4)
Produce	(10.6)	(6.5)	(8.6)
Dairy	2.6	(0.9)	1.7
All goods	(0.5)	(0.9)	(0.7)
Meat and produce excluded	(7.0)	1.2	4.0

Source. *Journal of Market Research* (August, 1969), p. 367, with permission.

By taking explicit account of quality he looks behind the raw statistics
and improves our understanding of apparent price differences.

FOOD QUALITY □ Reports of inferior quality cropped up in several
of the food price studies. They revealed evidence of wilted lettuce, fatty
hamburger, discolored meat, overripe fruit, and dented canned goods
in the lower income area stores—more so than in stores in middle- and
upper-income areas. Several factors could contribute to this condition:
poor merchandising, poor food handling, low turnover. None of the
studies charged that retailers deliberately stocked ghetto stores with
inferior meat and produce. In the New York, St. Louis, and Washington,
D.C. studies, representatives of three national food chains defended
their firms against the charge of inferior quality by stating that their
products were coded by number and shipped from central warehouses
with no opportunity to segregate the food according to quality.

The charge of inferior food quality in ghetto stores rests on the same scanty evidence that supports the assertion that the poor pay more for their food. The low-quality allegation cannot be quantified. Its confirmation depends upon visual inspection and the judgment of humans who are prone to error or whose prejudices may color their findings. Nonetheless, the available evidence seems to show that the quality of meat and produce in ghetto stores tends to lag behind that in other stores. It is just as important, however, to know the reasons for the condition as it is to know of its existence. Some doubt still exists on this score.

NONFOOD PRICES □ Earlier reference was made to *The Poor Pay More* by David Caplovitz.[12] This in-depth study of shopping conditions facing East Harlem residents criticized the "deviant marketing system" that served them. The research revealed that Caplovitz's ghetto subjects paid excessive prices for durable goods. Other studies confirm this finding; their results deserve further examination.

EAST HARLEM Caplovitz analyzed the marketing practices of retailers in East Harlem and the several hundred East Side New York families that patronized them. In summary, his research found that:

1. Lower income families (income under $3500/year) paid more than higher income families for television sets, record players, and washing machines.
2. Those shopping outside of the immediate neighborhood paid less than shoppers using local stores.
3. A related factor—higher appliance prices were associated more with traditional stores (neighborhood retailers), and lower prices with discount houses, chains, and department stores, which predominate outside of the ghetto.
4. Credit customers paid higher prices than cash customers.

The last factor created a greater burden for Negroes and Puerto Ricans than for whites. In the neighborhood stores, which thrive on credit sales, only 13% of the white credit customers paid what Caplovitz labels "high" prices while 56 to 69% of the Negro and Puerto Rican customers did. Interestingly, in the department, discount, and chain stores the percentages paying "high" prices were closer for the three groups. Caplovitz believes that this divergent pattern traces to

---

[12] David Caplovitz, *The Poor Pay More* (New York: The Free Press, 1967).

price standardization in the latter group of stores and their failure to adjust prices to account for race.

DISTRICT OF COLUMBIA STUDY[13]   The Federal Trade Commission surveyed 96 District of Columbia furniture and appliance retailers in 1966 to learn their installment credit and sales practices. The evidence showed the existence of much higher appliance prices in ghetto stores. "On the average, goods purchased for $100 at wholesale sold for $255 in the low-income market stores, compared with $159 in general market stores."[14] Table 6–2 indicates the range of price differences for eleven appliances. Prices for appliances sold by the low-income-area retailers ranged from 13 to 80% higher than prices at the department stores.

TABLE 6–2 Average "Retail Prices" of Appliances and Furniture for District of Columbia Retailers, 1966[a]

	Low-Income Market Retailers	General Market Retailers		
Product		Appliance Stores	Furniture Stores	Department Stores
Television set	$187	$131	$140	$134
Carpet	200	—	160	150
Refrigerator	202	132	133	153
Washing machine	204	133	148	155
Stereo-phonograph	211	149	157	153
Freezer	216	133	—	151
Dryer	217	135	138	160
Furniture	228	—	190	202
Vacuum cleaner	237	136	143	157
Radio	250	130	161	139
Sewing machine	297	196	—	174

[a] Assumes a wholesale price of $100. Prices based upon margin data revealed in survey.
Source. F.T.C. Survey.

Different average store sizes undoubtedly contributed to the price differences. Average annual sales for the general market retailers were

[13] Federal Trade Commission, *Economic Report on Installment Credit and Retail Sales Practices of District of Columbia Retailers,* reprinted in Frederick D. Sturdivant (ed.), *The Ghetto Marketplace* (New York: The Free Press, 1969), pp. 76–107.
[14] Ibid., p. 78.

seven times greater than they were for the ghetto stores. This condition ought to have affected costs—hence prices. Still, when the study matched ten low-income market retailers with ten equal-sized general retailers, large differences in gross margins continued to exist. They averaged 35.5% for the general market retailers, 62.2% for the low-income market retailers.

LOS ANGELES STUDY[15]   Sturdivant and Wilhelm looked beyond different prices charged in ghetto and nonghetto stores to study the effect of ethnicity on appliance prices. They arranged for three couples, white, Negro, and Mexican-American, to shop for television sets at stores in Culver City, Watts, and East Los Angeles. These areas are typical middle-class white, Negro, and Mexican-American, respectively, in Greater Los Angeles.

The findings are given below.

1. Average price quotations were higher by 17 to 48% in the two lower income areas than in the Culver City stores for four TV brands.
2. Installment credit costs tended to be higher when the couples shopped outside of their areas.
3. Minority couples were quoted higher prices than the white couple in two of the three white-area stores, but the prices were no greater than those in the ghetto stores and were often less. In other words, price discrimination was greater between location of store (ghetto versus nonghetto) than between ethnic group.

What do these studies add up to? Hardly *conclusive* evidence that the poor pay more for appliances. Still, what little evidence there is all points in the same direction—higher prices for the poor. All three surveys found that credit played an important part in the buying process in the ghetto stores. It influenced the effective prices substantially and also affected the ability of the poor to buy. With credit, too, comes a chain of relationships between ghetto merchant and his customer which contributes to the criticism of ghetto marketers.

GHETTO CREDIT PRACTICES ☐ The available data on credit use by

15 Frederick D. Sturdivant and Walter T. Wilhelm, "Poverty, Minorities, and Consumer Exploitation," reprinted in Sturdivant, op. cit., pp. 108–117.

the poor are mixed. Caplovitz found that about 60% of his East Harlem subjects had installment debts outstanding when he studied them.[16] This figure differed little from the percentage for all consumers. On the other hand, the F.T.C. study of ghetto shopping in Washington, D.C. revealed that 92.7% of the sales of stores in the low-income areas were installment sales; this compared with 26.5% for general market retailers outside of the ghettos.[17] These percentages are not necessarily inconsistent since some ghetto residents shop in nonghetto stores. We can infer from these figures—and other data support the inference— that many ghetto residents are trapped into using neighborhood stores for durable goods purchases. Here credit plays a dominant role in the buying process. Entrapment may take subtle forms. It results from the poor's relative lack of mobility, their lower level of education and inadequate information sources, and their lower income which puts many of them at the mercy of merchants who use credit as a prime selling tool. Thus, although the poor may incur no more installment debt than others, those who shop for durables in ghetto stores are almost certain to buy on time, with credit's attendant problems.

Caplovitz found that a majority of those he studied disliked the idea of incurring installment debt.[18] They objected to its high cost and they feared the prospect of repossession and garnishment. Their fears are not unfounded. The F.T.C. study revealed that 11 ghetto stores in 1960 filed 2690 judgments which resulted in 306 repossessions and 1568 garnishments; this compared with 16 repossessions and 35 garnishments for 12 nonghetto merchants.

Repossession and garnishment are standard practices by which ghetto retailers control their bad debt problem. Although customers suffer from them, they are not necessarily effective controls for the merchant. Repossession is often a weak device because of the shoddy character of many durables sold and the hard use often given them. Garnishment fails also when the customer is unemployed. Also, some employers will fire a worker rather than garnish his wages. As another stratagem, ghetto merchants frequently use lawsuits to recover bad debts. In Washington, D.C., 18 ghetto merchants studied by the F.T.C. filed 3030 suits for recovery of bad debts on $7.8 million in sales, an

16 Caplovitz, op. cit., p. 101.

17 Federal Trade Commission, *Economic Report on Installment Credit and Retail Sales Practices of District of Columbia Retailers,* March 1968, p. 23.

18 This finding differs from the results of a consumer study which shows a nation-wide sample of low-income consumers approving installment credit (George Katona, *The Powerful Consumer,* (New York: McGraw-Hill, 1960).)

average of one suit for every $2599 in sales.[19] Nonghetto stores studied sued only once for every $232,299 in sales. This device, too, may fail since many customers have no property to sue against, for recovery of the claim.

The merchants also have other ways available to control the bad debt problem without legal recourse. Some discount their installment credit paper with finance companies. This eliminates the problem, at a price, but it also reduces the retailers' control of relations with their customers. The finance company may sue to collect an unpaid debt but the merchant earns the customer's ill-will. The final weapon in the merchant's arsenal is what Caplovitz calls "informal control."[20] The merchants develop a social network of friends of customers who inform them of their customers' general welfare. When illness strikes a customer's family the merchant learns of it, and may adjust the payment schedule accordingly. Similarly, if other financial hardship hits the customer, for example, unemployment, the retailer may accept delayed payments. This leads to merchants operating on what is called "a 15-month year"—getting 12 payments spread over 15 months because of customers missing an average of one payment in four. A survey of ghetto credit disclosed that, despite this condition, the loss ratio for poor customers is not appreciably higher than it is for higher income groups.[21] Missing payments increased their delinquency rate but did not affect their final payment performance.

The proverbial "dollar down, dollar a week" accurately describes credit terms on ghetto retail transactions. Payments are low to reduce their burden. They are made often to keep close tabs on the customer and to get him into the store. Most customers visit the store to pay on their accounts. This arrangement gives the merchant repeated opportunities to make additional sales. This tying of the customer to a store is a familiar arrangement to many ghetto residents who have emigrated from the south. There, as sharecroppers, they had similar linkages with the company store.

The granting of credit is a major competitive tool for the ghetto merchant, and overshadows price as a determinant of sales, especially for hard goods. Credit exists in the sale of food but to a lesser extent than in the sale of durables. Some of the credit collection problems of ghetto merchants stem from their willingness to grant liberal credit terms as a

---

[19] Ibid., p. 26.
[20] Caplovitz, op. cit., p. 23.
[21] The National Urban Coalition, *Consumer Credit and the Low Income Consumer,* p. 4.

sales inducement. This behavior harms the improvident customer who gets deeply into debt. Thus the system gives both customer and seller a tool with which each can satisfy a need, but it simultaneously creates problems for them both.

Unfortunately for the customer, most of the cards are stacked against him. The merchants possess more market knowledge, better access to legal remedies, and the ability, through obfuscation, to extract credit terms that compensate them for the risk they incur. Many ghetto shoppers lack the knowledge and, often, reading ability to realize the credit terms they have agreed to when they make a durable goods purchase. Congressional hearings reveal numerous instances of ghetto shoppers being unaware of having to pay finance charges even though the papers that they signed indicated a total cost in excess of the price quoted them.[22]

The ghetto shopper pays dearly for his use of credit. Sturdivant and Wilhelm report their experimental shoppers being quoted prices, including credit charges, for TV sets that ran up to 87% above the regular list price.[23] The F.T.C. study reveals average annual finance charges of 23 to 25% in ghetto stores, four percentage points above the rates in nonghetto stores.[24]

GHETTO MERCHANT PRACTICES □ The low-income shopper suffers from more than the extortionate finance charges imposed by ghetto merchants. He is victimized by other merchant practices.[25] Often durable goods have no price marks. The price may hinge upon whether the shopper is judged a good or bad credit risk. The same phenomenon occurred in the shopping study in Watts, East Los Angeles, and Culver City. Price also depends on the assumed naïveté of the shopper. Sales personnel become adept at measuring the economic status of their customers. Salesmen may refer high credit risk shoppers to other stores specializing in such accounts—at higher prices. The store making the referral receives a kickback commission. Most furniture and appliance stores also lack high-quality merchandise since the use of high percentage markups would price quality merchandise out of the market.

A widespread and nefarious ghetto merchant practice, reported by Caplovitz and others, is the use of bait and switch techniques. They

[22] Homer Kripke, "Gesture and Reality in Consumer Credit Reform," reprinted in Aaker and Day (eds.), op. cit., p. 161.
[23] Sturdivant and Wilhelm, op. cit., p. 114.
[24] Federal Trade Commission, op. cit., p. 26.
[25] See Caplovitz, op. cit.

take several forms. The "bait" may be an attractively priced bedroom suite displayed in the store's windows. Inside, the shopper is pressured into buying higher priced items. Merchandise in the window display is "unavailable" or "incomplete." The bait may take the form of an ad for a bargain. Attracted to the store, the customer again is high pressured into buying another, more expensive model.

Ghetto customers also complain of being quoted one price and signing sales contracts containing higher prices. They may reluctantly pay the higher price or make the down payment, refuse to make additional payments, finally default and lose the merchandise. Equally nefarious is the tactic of switching goods after the sale. Here the customer pays for a new item and receives a used or reconditioned model. The ways to defraud the gullible customer appear endless.

Bait and switch tactics may not be used more in the ghetto than elsewhere, but their use may be morally more reprehensible for two reasons. Ghetto residents generally have less than average education and therefore may be more susceptible to deceptive persuasion. Also their financial straits magnify the impact of unwise buying decisions.

ROLE OF THE PEDDLER □ An adjunct to the ghetto marketing system is the peddler who serves several functions. He may act as the merchant's bird dog, canvassing the neighborhood for prospects. Not only does he prod reluctant shoppers to patronize the merchant but he also forms an important communication link between the retailer and the ghetto resident. By insinuating himself into the home, he gets to know the family, its economic condition, its problems and needs and, importantly, its credit-worthiness. Often he operates independently from the merchant on a commission arrangement, or he may act as a dealer, buying from a retailer at a "wholesale" price. Caplovitz saw the peddler as responsible for much of the exploitation among the East Harlem residents he studied.

Ghetto shoppers use the peddler extensively. Over one-half of Caplovitz' sample had bought from a peddler at least once. Only one shopper in ten considered his relationship with the peddler to be satisfactory. Many transactions involved were impulse purchases, responding to the hawker's persuasion. Usually he succeeded because he offered credit that other merchants refused to grant. His willingness to supply credit freely is his stock-in-trade and provides his principal differential advantage.

SHOPPING BEHAVIOR OF THE POOR □ It is evident that the poor are heavily dependent on credit and often succumb to the wiles of rapacious merchants. What other buying characteristics do they exhibit? Louise G. Richards compares their buying behavior with the "rational" practices of careful shoppers.[26] Good consumership involves:

1. Buying necessities first, luxuries last. According to Richards, the poor generally do this. They tend to buy basics first, and consume fewer durables.[27] They may appear to spend more than they actually do on durables because of their conspicuous consumption of television sets. Given their limited expenditures on recreation, should one classify TV as a luxury or a necessity? Symbolism enters into other purchases of the poor. The working class wife dreams of a modern kitchen not only for its labor-saving features as a middle-class wife might, but as a symbolic end in itself. Negro families consume twice as much Scotch—a high-status drink—as do whites.[28] Caplovitz refers to this behavior as "compensatory consumption," which is the equivalent for low-income people of Veblen's conspicuous consumption.[29]

2. Getting the best quality at the lowest price. The poor score poorly on this count. They are less inclined to search for lower prices, are less well informed, and less willing to buy used items. Although the percentage of the poor with installment debt may be no greater than for other income groups, the *burden* of the debt may be more severe since their debt-income ratio is higher. Their failure to seek bargains and their inferior knowledge of market conditions probably stem from their lower level of education. The recent migrant status of many blacks and Puerto Ricans contributes to their problem. They tend to shop close to home in personalized surroundings until they get acclimated to their new environment. This lack of mobility reduces their purchase options and minimizes their market knowledge. On

---

[26] Louise G. Richards, "Consumer Practices of the Poor," in Sturdivant, *The Ghetto Marketplace,* op. cit., pp. 42–60.

[27] We need to treat these generalizations with caution. First, they suffer the disadvantages of all generalizations. Second, generalizations about the poor often are confused with generalizations about Negroes. Raymond A. Bauer and Scott M. Cunningham, (*Studies in the Negro Market* (Cambridge, Mass., Marketing Science Institute, 1970)) show the disparity between consumption patterns for whites and blacks with the same income. We associate blacks with the ghetto and low-income areas; yet, low-income whites outnumber low-income blacks 2 to 1.

[28] Richards, op. cit., p. 48.

[29] Caplovitz, op. cit., p. 13. He borrows the term from Robert K. Merton.

the other hand, Richards indicates that the poor tend to shop for specials in the purchase of durables, and the *very* poor are inclined to buy goods on sale—practices that give them high marks for good consumership.

3. Budgeting incomes and planning purchases ahead. Again the poor show up poorly. Many of them have a negative net worth. Their lack of education affects their knowledge of money management. Planning suffers too when the immediate assumes overriding importance as it does for those who live a hand-to-mouth existence. Richards reports a study showing that education is more important than income in predicting planning propensities.[30] The poor's lower education level may reduce their ability to conceive of the abstraction of deferred spending when immediate gratification seems infinitely more rewarding and perhaps even necessary for survival.

4. Meeting needs through home production. The poor seem to rely less on home growing of food and home repairs than others. Living in crowded urban housing and owning fewer homes partly account for these tendencies. Education is another contributing factor. Home production depends in part upon acquiring skills and training that many poor lack. The cost of acquiring tools also deters them.

5. Taking advantage of consumer benefits. Legal, medical, and other agencies are available to the poor, but Richards reports that they fail to use them as much as they might to relieve their financial plight.

Running through these behavioral patterns are several common threads. First is fatalism, a life theme that leads to resignation to one's condition. Related to this is the poor's orientation to the present, which calls for more immediate gratification of impulses and less planning for the future. They are also less mobile, physically and socially. Confined by tradition and lack of transportation to their neighborhood, the poor are less well equipped to "shop around." Less willingness to deal with strangers contributes to this condition. Social restrictions (immobility) heighten the desire for status objects and entertainment alternatives—hence, the tendency toward compensatory consumption. This behavior points up another characteristic—concreteness, or stress-

[30] Richards, op. cit., p. 55.

ing material over intellectual things. Underlying most of their behavior is the pervading influence of education. Inadequate education lies at the heart of many of the poor's marketing problems. In part, it accounts for their being bilked by unscrupulous merchants. It limits their knowledge of market opportunities. It reduces their access to agencies and information which would improve their bargain-hunting batting average and would help to bail them out of the unpleasant aftermath of unwise purchases.[31] Most important, better education should beget more income which could do much to relieve their downtrodden condition.

SUGGESTED REMEDIES □ How can we reform the ghetto marketing system to make it more responsive to the poor's needs? First we must establish what those needs are. Mary Gardiner Jones of the Federal Trade Commission suggests the need for: (1) more market information; (2) more choice, both in merchandise and in credit (to reduce the poor's dependence on specific merchants); (3) more flexible credit to allow ghetto shoppers to miss installment credit payments without running the danger of foreclosure; and (4) more counseling, sympathetic advice, and concern from merchants to relieve their anxieties about shopping in large, depersonalized stores.[32] Obviously, ghetto shoppers need a couple of other reforms: the availability of higher quality merchandise and lower prices.

Before examining possible remedies, it might be well to see what handicaps face existing ghetto marketers. Prevailing conditions may limit reforms that feasibly can be implemented.

Ghetto merchants and chain-store executives argue that conditions peculiar to the ghetto cause prices to rise. Among these conditions are higher pilferage rates, higher insurance costs arising out of vandalism and mistreatment of equipment, elevated land costs and rents, lower total sales volume which increases overhead costs per unit, and smaller purchases per customer in food stores.[33] Evidence also indicates that

---

[31] "When asked where they would go for help if they were being cheated by a merchant or salesman, almost two-thirds of the low-income consumers interviewed replied that they did not know." (Eric Schnapper, "Consumer Legislation and the Poor," in Aaker and Day (eds.), op. cit., p. 343.)

[32] Mary Gardiner Jones, "Deception in the Marketplace of the Poor: The Role of the Federal Trade Commission," in Sturdivant (ed.), op. cit., p. 253–254.

[33] "Because the per capita sale in an inner-city store averages only one half of the typical sale in a suburban store, more help is needed to serve twice as much traffic to ring up the same sales dollars. The wear and tear on the store and its fixtures are also more a result of traffic than of sales volume." Donald S. Perkins,

ghetto stores have a problem of recruiting and maintaining competent management personnel, and this factor is bound to affect costs. Less vigorous competition in ghetto retailing is a noncost element that also must influence prices. Many low-income areas lack the stimulation of chain store supermarket competition. The reduced mobility of ghetto residents and their attachment to local stores where service is personalized limit shopping alternatives, with a consequent reduction in competitive pressure.

Donald S. Perkins says that attempts to cut the cost of food in retailing in the ghetto leads to an irony. "Most of the efforts to make sure that the poor don't pay more, may in fact be insuring that the poor will pay more."[34] Perkins, president of a food retailing chain, claims that multichain-store operators with ghetto stores try to charge the same prices in the ghetto that they do outside. Evidence from the Congressional hearings on ghetto food prices reveals the same pattern. Operating with higher costs, ghetto stores suffer a price-cost squeeze. Perkins claims that the squeeze has eliminated profits for many chain stores and left others only marginally profitable. The result: abandonment of stores, which leaves the field open to smaller, high-cost operations. Hence the irony.

Actual cost data on ghetto retailing operations are scarce. The comparative study of furniture and appliance dealers in and out of the ghetto in Washington, D.C., provides some information on this score. Table 6–3 summarizes the data. The wide disparity in gross margins accounts for the big price differentials between the two classes of stores. A small part of the difference traces to different profit margins. Higher salary and commission expense in the ghetto stores result from their greater use of door-to-door commission salesmen who also double as bill collectors. "Other" expenses include administration and delivery expenses, costs of processing credit, interest on borrowed funds, legal and insurance costs. Given the character of ghetto retail operations, one can understand why low-income stores' costs are higher. The larger bad debt loss figure for ghetto stores appears to contradict earlier evidence that the loss ratio was not appreciably higher for the poor than for higher income people. Even if the loss figure is only a little higher, the concentration of low-income shoppers' sales in ghetto stores and their much lower relative patronage of nonghetto stores would

"The Low-Income Consumer—A Human Problem and a Selling Problem," speech in Executive Lecture Series, University of Notre Dame, March 2, 1970.
  [34] Perkins, ibid.

TABLE 6–3 Comparison of Expenses and Profits for Low-Income and General Market Retailers of Furniture and Appliances in Washington, D.C., 1966

	Percent of Sales			
Revenue Component	10 Low-Income Retailers ($5,146,395)[c]		10 General Market Retailers ($5,405,221)[c]	
Operating ratio as percent of sales	100.0		100.0	
Cost of goods sold	37.8		64.5	
Gross profit margin	62.2		35.5	
Salary and commission expense[a]		28.2		17.8
Advertising expense		2.1		3.9
Bad debt losses		6.7		0.3
Other expenses[b]		21.3		11.2
Total expenses	58.3		33.2	
Net return on sales	3.9		2.3	

[a] Includes officers' salaries.
[b] Other expenses, including taxes, after deductions of other income.
[c] 1966 sales.

Source. Federal Trade Commission, "Economic Report on Installment Credit and Retail Sales Practices of District of Columbia Retailers," March 1968, p. 18.

exaggerate the difference in bad debt costs. Less use of citywide advertising media by ghetto merchants accounts for their lower ad costs.

The most significant feature of Table 6–3 is the fairly narrow difference in profit margins for the two classes of stores. Critics tend to associate higher prices with higher profits. This example is not conclusive, but it contradicts the usual impression. A larger sample of the Washington, D.C., stores revealed similar findings. Data on rates of return on stockholders' equity were mixed. For the larger sample of stores they give the edge to the nonghetto stores; for the 20-store sample covered in Table 6–3, rates of return on equity for the ghetto stores were 12.7% compared with 8.1% for the general market retailers.[35] These data suffer from serious limitations. The cooperating stores used nonuniform accounting practices. Even if they are only approximate, they shed some light on an area that is shrouded in suspicion. The absence of abnormally high profits for the ghetto stores

[35] Federal Trade Commission, op. cit., p. 21. The data covered only 9 of the 10 nonghetto stores.

should not surprise us. Given reasonably free entry conditions, abnormal profits should induce entrants into trade. This should damp down prices and restore a normal profit equilibrium.

Considering the higher risk conditions that exist in the ghetto, merchants there ought to expect the reward of higher profits. If other profit margin data revealed that profits in the ghetto exceeded those outside the ghetto, critics legitimately ought to show that they are greater than necessary to compensate for the added risk if they are to substantiate their charges of gouging. It is unfortunate that so little cost- and profit-margin data exist to help evaluate the competitive performance of ghetto retailing. Most studies emphasize prices. Until we have more complete profit comparisons and a better idea of appropriate risk premiums for operating in the inner city, we cannot competently judge performance there.

Having examined some of the cost constraints facing ghetto merchants, how can they be overcome? A suggested remedy for higher prices in the ghetto is the construction of more supermarkets. Of course, they already exist in many locations. But critics of present ghetto marketing practices would like to see more. They feel that too many low-income residents are dependent for food purchases upon small, inefficient retailers. Some chains have decided against entering the ghetto. A number of factors discourage them, some already mentioned. In addition to cost factors, they are deterred by the ghetto's low purchasing power and the difficulty of acquiring large store sites that will accommodate adequate parking facilities. High risks associated with the threat of arson, riots, vandalism, and pilferage also trouble many chain operators.

Suggested corrections take several forms, usually involving some kind of government intervention. Sturdivant proposes an investment guarantee plan to encourage investment in the ghetto. It would protect retailers against losses from riots, arson, looting, and other manifestations of civil unrest.[36] The guarantee would reimburse merchants not only for physical damage but also for loss of profits. An assessment based on the value of insured assets would provide funds for reimbursing losses. This proposal would cover all ghetto retail operations and not just food stores. Sturdivant would couple the arrangement with a proviso cancelling the guarantee if a retailer violated laws designed to protect consumers, for example, if installment loan interest ceilings

[36] Frederick D. Sturdivant, "Better Deal for the Ghetto Shoppers," in Sturdivant (ed.), op. cit., p. 153.

were exceeded. The guarantee would insure against the added investment risks in the ghetto. To compensate for higher costs, Sturdivant
would offer investment tax credits. It is hard to imagine how this incentive would help the retailer who is unable to earn a profit because of
his elevated costs.

Others suggest tax incentives and investment guarantees.[37] Among
additional suggested remedies to make new retailing investments in the
inner city more attractive are lower insurance rates (presumably through
government subsidy), better police protection, the arrangement for non-
cancellable insurance policies, and provision for land clearance for
store sites.

Perkins suggests a unique subsidy scheme to encourage the introduction of large food stores into the ghetto in spite of higher costs there.
He would offer the merchant the subsidy in return for his banking food
stamps that were spent in his store. This not only induces the merchant
to serve an area that he might shun without the subsidy but it also encourages the merchant to woo the poor—a refreshing contrast to the
existing situation. Undoubtedly, subsidies could take other forms. This
is only one example of their use. Subsidies can be effective in encouraging economic activity which, in their absence, would not occur; however, they may induce an "inefficient" allocation of resources. They
call forth activity that does not occur in response to normal market
forces. Their use requires a public policy determination that their benefits exceed the possible inefficiencies in resource allocation that their
use may create.[38]

Will these various proposals induce lower cost outside retailers to
set up shop in the ghetto? There is previously cited evidence of their
skepticism. How about black entrepreneurs? How will they respond to
incentives? Critics contend that a major problem with the ghetto marketing structure is the dominant ownership of inner city retail stores by
whites. "Blacks run and operate less than 1 percent of the five million
private businesses in the country."[39] They see exorbitant retail prices

[37] For example, see "Should Supermarkets Take a New Look at Urban Areas?"
in Sturdivant (ed.), op. cit., p. 180.

[38] We need to stress the *possible* inefficient allocation of resources. Whether it is
efficient or inefficient depends on the cost functions that result from the subsidies'
use. They may create a situation in which the scale of output is enlarged sufficiently
to move the firm down its long-run cost curve, hence improve its technical efficiency.

[39] Urban America and the Urban Coalition, *One Year Later—An Assessment of
the Nation's Response to the Crisis Described by the National Advisory Commission on Civil Disorders,* reported in Nathan Glazer, *"The Missing Bootstrap,"
Saturday Review* (August 23, 1969), p. 21.

and extortionate credit charges as manifestations of white economic dominance of blacks. Why not increase the blacks' control over retail institutions that serve them? In this way profits will stay in the community rather than drain off to the white suburbs.

Black capitalism lies at the heart of attempts to reduce black economic dependence on whites. The concept encompasses the ownership of both retail and manufacturing operations. It usually envisions the black-owned firms operating in the ghetto. With blacks owning equity, hiring blacks, and serving blacks, the black community ought to gain. Indigenous ownership should overcome some limitations in the existing marketing system. This is the hope. Is it realistic?

The concept of black capitalism is not new.[40] Businesses owned by blacks have existed for some time, both in and out of the ghetto. What is new is the attempt to accelerate the movement of black ownership and management of trade and industry. The payout from increased black capitalism could be substantial. It could take the form of increased employment for blacks, increased economic benefits from wages and profits retained in the ghetto, and enhanced racial pride. These are worthwhile potential benefits.

But there are also drawbacks to the concept of black capitalism. Charles Silberman criticizes the emphasis of Theodore Cross and others on blacks operating in the ghetto to serve the ghetto's needs.[41] In our history, ethnic groups have benefited from this practice. But, Silberman contends, they soon branched out to serve broader markets. Examples are the Jews in the clothing trade, Armenians in carpets, and the Irish in construction. Silberman believes that the operation of ghetto businesses by blacks confuses the goals of rehabilitating decrepit urban business areas and uplifting the blacks' economic position with the goal of increasing the number of black businessmen. The latter goal contributes to the first two but they are not the same.

A major barrier to the advancement of black capitalism is the environment in which it must operate. Changing ownership from white to black will not eradicate the problems facing existing merchants—high pilferage rates, vandalism, the threat of riots and, most importantly, the depressed income level of the ghetto inhabitants. It is not an exaggeration to say that inner city market areas are underdeveloped enclaves within

40 See Theodore L. Cross, *Black Capitalism: Strategy for Business in the Ghetto* (New York: Atheneum, 1969) for interesting proposals to expand black capitalism.
41 Charles E. Silberman, "What Ever Became of Black Capitalism?" *Fortune* (August 1970), pp. 197–198.

a developed economy. They suffer from the same absence of purchasing power that plagues less developed countries. They are also short of the management talent necessary for successful business operations. Mortality in retailing is high to begin with. Will the encouragement of black entrepreneurship in low-income areas increase the prospects for failure for a group that desperately needs and deserves more successes? It is this need to recognize the realities of ghetto conditions that leads critics of black capitalism to urge caution in its adoption.

Black capitalism advocates view banking as a fertile and useful service field for blacks to cultivate. Controlling their own financial institutions would give blacks a measure of autonomy that they now lack. It ought to provide additional benefits. Caplovitz views the establishment of banks in the ghettos as a way to attract savings so residents there will save and buy for cash rather than for credit.[42] Black-owned banks and finance companies might also handle ghetto residents' credit needs more sympathetically than is presently the case.

Low-income people already receive some credit assistance through the establishment of limited income, federal credit unions.[43] At the end of 1968, 669 of these institutions existed. Their assets totaled $30 million; loans outstanding amounted to $22 million. Thus their impact is minimal. Still they offer a vehicle to meet the credit needs of the poor and to induce saving. Groups whose median income lies below $3000 a year or certain groups occupying public housing are eligible to belong to the credit organization.

Some retailers and banks also offer the poor assistance to ease their credit problems. These services include short courses on the use of credit as well as consumer education. Greater knowledge by low-income consumers of various facets of the buying process would undoubtedly improve their lot. Too often they suffer from inadequate knowledge of credit terms, product quality, and shopping alternatives available to them. Supporters of "truth-in-lending" legislation hope that fuller disclosure of finance charges will aid low-income shoppers.[44] As noted in Chapter 5, this may be a vain hope.

There is a self-help project designed to remedy the high food cost problem that offers promise. This is the growing development of consumer co-ops in the ghettos—as well as in middle class housing areas. Aided by Office of Economic Opportunity personnel, buying clubs

[42] Caplovitz, op. cit., p. 187.
[43] See The National Urban Coalition, op. cit., p. 28, for a description of this institution.
[44] Federal Trade Commission, op. cit., p. xiv.

are being formed through Community Action Centers.[45] Others form from the impetus of individuals who live in housing developments or apartment complexes and who seek a way to lower their food bills. Members of the club chip into a fund that is used to buy large quantities of food at wholesale prices. Buying duties rotate among the members. Advocates of buying co-ops claim that members reduce food bills significantly and obtain higher quality products. Cox and Seidman report that of the ghetto co-ops they studied, some were operating successfully, and some were not.[46] Skeptics doubt their durability, noting that a similar movement (fad?) existed 30 years ago.[47] Most lasted only a few months.

SUMMARY AND CONCLUSIONS ☐ Whether the poor pay more for food is far from clear. The evidence is mixed. When one adjusts for quality and the size of stores available to the poor, the evidence points toward higher prices in the ghetto. Conclusive statements depend upon conclusive findings. Much of the available research involves studies of a few stores in a limited number of cities. Some of the research lacked adequate controls. For example, the stores covered in the B.L.S. research had advance notice of the price study, and only those consenting to be studied were analyzed. There are other problems. One of the stickiest is getting comparable market baskets in ghetto and nonghetto stores since these shops often fail to carry identical brands. Different product preferences for various ethnic and racial groups also lead to stores stocking different items.

The studies of ghetto food prices tend to agree on one thing: the limited availability of high-volume food chain operations in low-income areas. They exist, but not to the extent that they do elsewhere. This shortcoming puts the ghetto resident at a definite disadvantage in his food buying.

In nonfood retailing, the poor are disadvantaged in several important ways. Forced to rely on credit, they often become victimized both by unscrupulous merchants and by their ignorance of commercial practices. A number of existing and potential remedies exist: better credit

---

[45] "Should Supermarkets Take a New Look at Urban Areas?" in Sturdivant (ed.), op. cit., p. 178.

[46] William E. Cox, Jr. and Sue R. Seidman, "Cooperatives in the Ghetto," in Philip R. McDonald (ed.), *Marketing Involvement in Society and the Economy*, American Marketing Association, Proceedings of Fall Conference (Cincinnati, Ohio, 1969), p. 42.

[47] "Food Shoppers Buy Together," *Business Week* (December 5, 1970), p. 99.

facilities and information, indigenously owned retail and service institutions, the introduction of more low-cost retail institutions, and investment and insurance guarantees to stimulate the creation of new institutions.

Some of the suggested reforms may fail to account for structural conditions in the ghetto that are not easily modified. For a while at least, ghetto businesses must continue to face high-cost, high-risk conditions and must serve an economically depressed clientele. These handicaps reduce the potential effectiveness of efforts designed to reform ghetto marketing. The higher success rate for franchised operations offers hope that this form of organization may overcome some of the traditional problems associated with small-scale retailing. Franchising offers an increasingly attractive route to advance black capitalism with a greater prospect of success than it has previously enjoyed.

Despite drawbacks to the present ghetto marketing system, it still performs in a way that meets the needs of its users. Caplovitz describes the ghetto marketing system as "in many respects a deviant one, in which unethical and illegal practices abound. Nevertheless," he says, "it can persist because it fulfills social functions that are presently not fulfilled by more legitimate institutions."[48] The peddler's granting of high-cost credit to those denied credit elsewhere is a case in point. Still, concerned observers wonder whether the poor cannot share more fully than they have in the fruits of low-cost and ethical marketing which others more fortunate than they receive without hindrance.

□ DISCUSSION QUESTIONS □

1. There seems to be some uncertainty as to whether ghetto-area food prices are or are not higher than nonghetto food prices. Draw up a research design that would answer this question.

2. What role should government play to improve ghetto marketing conditions?

3. Assume that you are president of a large retail food chain. You are concerned about inadequate supermarket facilities in the ghettos but you are also concerned about adverse operating conditions there,

48 Caplovitz, op. cit., p. 180.

for example, high pilferage rates and high insurance costs. What recommendations would you make to your Board of Directors concerning the opening of stores in those areas?

4. Does business have an obligation to black merchants to help them establish and maintain viable business operations? If so, what form should the assistance take?

5. "Risks are higher in the ghetto than they are outside of the ghetto, therefore businesses operating there deserve higher rates of return." Evaluate.

6. Evaluate the "Black Capitalism" concept. What benefits might result from its increased use? Any disadvantages?

7. Many ghetto retailers victimize shoppers with "bait and switch" selling tactics. Define the term. As a consumer, have you been exposed to this approach? Describe the situation.

8. Can legislation feasibly limit the use of bait and switch tactics? How would it work?

9. What obligation, if any, does the municipal government have to improve ghetto marketing conditions?

Index